PANIC AZIMUTH

A Senior Leader's Guide to Building Trust, Discipline, and High-Performing Teams

This photo was taken of me when I was at Light Leaders Course at Ft Benning, GA. I was using the sun as a reference point to quicky assess my azimuth. If I used a "hang loose" lining up my pinky finger with the sun and my thumb as the azimuth, I was right on azimuth. LT Paul Swanson, who took the photo, was skeptical until we landed right on our point.

Dedication

For the Highlanders of the 1st Battalion 161st Infantry.

First in War, First in Peace

Foreword

There's something about riding in a convoy with someone that accelerates the process of getting to know them. Maybe it's the need to shout over the roar of the engine or check their blind spots, but that left-seat-right-seat dynamic mirrors the leadership relationships within the Armed Services. It's not always perfect, and it doesn't always make for lifelong relationships, but for me, that first ride with Dan Massey sealed it. One convoy, and we were locked in for life.

Dan's leadership wasn't just about his technical skills or his ability to execute. It was his unshakable belief in those around him, his ability to teach through example, and his focus on making everyone around him better. His passion was the same whether he was supporting his peers, his soldiers, or myself. To describe his leadership as tenacious and confident would be an understatement, it was transformative in measurable ways.

The undertone in this work carries the passion for the true form of leadership; a desire to help those around you and those that come after you. This book is not intended to be a script to follow but a perspective for company grade leadership to consider when trying to achieve effective results. Dan's insights weren't about a one-size-fits-all approach but about carving a path that works for you, your soldiers, and your organization, and your mission, with whatever resources you have at your disposal. It was through Dan's insights that I was successful as a junior leader, and through his leadership that our soldiers' lives improved.

The lessons in this book are those that Dan shared with me during our convoys, after arduous field operations, or in late-night conversations as we wrapped up drills. These are lessons born of real-world application, tested and refined through experience. This book isn't just a toolkit. It's a guide to navigating the complexities of leadership at the company level and beyond, providing the insights and tools necessary to lead with confidence and purpose.

Stefan T. D. Williams, Ph.D.

CPT, IN

Panic Azimuth
Publishing

Acknowledgements

To the leaders of the 81st Brigade and the 1st Battalion, 161st Infantry, thank you for the privilege of serving alongside you and for entrusting me to lead within this extraordinary formation. To my family, Renee, Emmy, and Evan, your support throughout my years in the Army has been my foundation, and I am forever grateful. And to every Soldier I have had the honor of serving with, thank you for your service, your professionalism, and your unwavering dedication to the profession of arms.

Prologue

I became the First Sergeant (1SG) of Bravo Company, 1-161 Infantry. After years of serving as a Platoon Sergeant, I believed I was ready. I spent a significant amount of time in this company, not only as a Platoon Sergeant but also as the Company Readiness Noncommissioned Officer (NCO). I knew the Soldiers, the rhythm of the unit, and the unit's personality and culture. Serving as the company's Readiness NCO, you gain intimate administrative knowledge of the formation. I knew every Soldier by first name.

Like many of us before stepping into a new challenge, I walked in with confidence, the kind built on experience and familiarity.

That confidence didn't last long.

During one of my first battalion training meetings, the Battalion Commander asked a series of questions that a seasoned First Sergeant should have been able to answer without hesitation. I couldn't. The truth hit me; I wasn't as prepared as I thought I was, and I felt like a failure in that moment. That was the first of many moments in my new role where I walked away convinced I was failing as a First Sergeant.

I realized quickly that stepping into the First Sergeant role wasn't just a promotion; it was a complete transformation. The strengths and habits that made me successful as a Platoon Sergeant didn't automatically translate upward. The margin for error shrank, and the expectations multiplied. Suddenly, I was navigating unfamiliar territory without a failsafe, no seasoned 1SG to fall back on, no safety net to catch my missteps. Every decision carried more weight; every hesitation had consequences. It was up to me now; I was the First Sergeant. The responsibility I once shared now rested entirely on my shoulders, and there was no one left to point to for backup, correction, or reassurance.

Sure, you've got a Company Commander (CO), a Command Sergeant Major (CSM), and peer First Sergeants around you. But in reality, quality time for guidance from any of them is scarce. Once you're running a company, that time gets swallowed by your primary mission, leading your people, solving problems, and training a company. Mentorship opportunities dry up fast. You're the one expected to provide it now, not receive it.

Here's a perspective to consider. Most of your bosses and peers are wrestling with the same doubts and uneasiness in their own roles, at every level. Leadership at this level—and above—can feel incredibly lonely: everyone's figuring it out on the fly, often in silence. Just be ready to be on your own. And that's okay. It's part of the job.

The good news is that recognizing it is the first step. Many leaders find actual relief by quietly building a small circle of trusted peers or mentors outside their immediate chain. Conversely, many come to see that same solitude as a valuable space for clearer thinking, independent judgment, and resilience. Ultimately, it's how you frame the isolation—whether as a burden or an asset—that shapes your experience. Both perspectives can be valid, depending on the moment and how you choose to use it.

If you go searching for a manual on how to be a successful Company First Sergeant, you won't find one. Doctrine, policy, and leadership theory are every-where, and all of them matter. I studied them, relied on them, and believed they had prepared me. But none of them fully captured what it felt like sitting in the hot seat, to feel the impact of responsibility settle in, or to wrestle with the quiet doubt that follows the realization that you are now accountable for everything the company does, or fails to do, and for every Soldier entrusted to you. Experience gave me confidence, but stepping into that role brought something different: clarity about the gravity of the responsibility and the leader the job demanded me to become.

I recall speaking with another new first sergeant when I first took the role.

"Brother, I feel like we're two blind men trying to guide each other through a cactus patch," I said.

He laughed mostly because he felt the same way.

It is common to feel unprepared when stepping into a new role as a senior leader. No matter how accomplished you are, the transition can awaken quiet uncertainty. That inner voice, the one that whispers you are not ready, that you will fail, that you are not good enough, can be relentless. Just know that you're human and this is common.

Just know, that negative inner voice is an asshole!

Left unchecked, it will erode confidence and distort perspective. But it can also be redirected. Instead of allowing doubt to paralyze you, harness it. Reframe the question from *"What if I do it wrong?"* to *"What can I do better?"* Shift from *"I'm not good enough"* to *"How can I elevate this team and myself?"*

Self-doubt, when disciplined, becomes self-assessment. And self-assessment is a hallmark of strong leadership. The goal is not to silence the voice entirely, but to transform it, so that it fuels growth, sharpens awareness, and ultimately makes both you and your organization better.

I completed my tour as the B Company First Sergeant with one simple goal: if I walked away today, the company had to be better than when I found it. I was not a perfect First Sergeant by any means. In truth, I struggled through my first command, as most do. There were moments of uncertainty, hard lessons learned in real time, and decisions I made that I wish I could take back. Looking at my struggles now, they were not setbacks; they were essential steps in my development.

Years later, long after I'd packed up my office and moved on from Bravo Company, my phone buzzed with a number I recognized instantly. It was the Battalion Sergeant Major. That man never called just to chat; if your phone lit up with his name, something was on fire or about to be.

I answered, and the first thing I heard was his tone, that heavy, controlled inhale leaders take right before they drop something big on you.

"Brother... Bravo Company's in trouble," he said.

It didn't surprise me. Even though I'd moved on and was serving as the Charlie Company First Sergeant, you can't escape the pulse of a battalion. You hear things, the grumblings in the hallway, the sidelong comments at the chow hall, the unofficial back-channel warnings about leadership going sideways. Soldiers always know when a unit is struggling, and those whispers had been getting louder for months.

He got straight to the point.

"They need direction. You're the best man for the job."

I actually laughed out loud, a true LOL. I thought he was messing with me. *Nobody* goes back to the same company as a First Sergeant, not twice. It's an unwritten rule: you get one shot at it, then you move on, and the unit becomes someone else's problem or someone else's success story.

But then he said, "No, I'm serious. Pack your stuff. I need you back in the B-Co 1SG seat."

It was one of those moments where the only right answer is, "Roger that, Sergeant Major."

After that phone call, and allowing some time for the information to sink in. I reflected on the first time I took Bravo Company as the 1SG, the doubt, the uncertainty, the long nights wondering if I was screwing it up more than I was helping. I remembered the faces of Soldiers who deserved better than the version of me they got. This time around, I was ready!

Walking back into that company area felt surreal. The building was new, but I certainly wasn't. Most Soldiers recognized me instantly. A few gave me the classic *"Oh no... he's back"* look. Others stared with that half-squint, trying to place me, like a familiar ghost wandering through the hallway.

However, this time, I wasn't coming back as the unsure First Sergeant I'd once been. I wasn't searching for an azimuth.

I was stepping in to give one.

Weeks before I ever stepped foot inside the company area, I called every squad leader to let them know I was returning to Bravo Company. Their responses were what I expected. Every one of them sounded relieved, even excited. Only later did I learn I had unknowingly derailed a full-blown mutiny in the making. The squad leaders had reached their breaking point and were planning to leave Bravo Company en masse, spreading that message down to their Soldiers. Morale had not simply decreased. It was destroyed.

The simple phone call I had with all the squad leaders shows that a simple act can have a profound impact. It prompted all the squad leaders to communicate with each other and adjust their plans to stay, and best of all, they shared the good news with their squad members! A brief phone call led to an overwhelming victory.

I planned to push every aspect of culture building I could muster. I knew full well that some of my methods would not be well-liked by the higher command. But I was not put there to boost the commands ego, I was there to boost the egos of B-Co Soldiers. They were my focus and whom I needed to impress. I will never forget that first formation after my Change of Responsibility to Bravo Company.

It was just me and my new company, under-manned and hurting from a series of poor leadership. We were B-Co, and I said to the men in a low but commanding tone,

"When I call you to attention, you sound off with Bastards."

I called the unit to attention, and when they sounded off, the windows rattled and the walls shook. I knew it was game on! Leadership really does come full circle. At least it did for me.

The "Bastard" story warrants a bit of context. Years earlier, during my first run as the First Sergeant of Company B (then Bold Company), I tried renaming us the "Bold Bastards," but the idea stayed on ice. Years later, when the battalion launched its Highlander-themed renaming campaign—Axe, Broadsword, Claymore, and Halberd for HHC—I spotted my opening. A bastard sword is a type of broadsword, so the name fit perfectly. No, I wasn't calling anyone fatherless... well, maybe a bit. What mattered was the edge, history, and attitude it captured for our outfit. It became our war cry, something to rally behind when things got kinetic. The men loved it, and they had the only vote that counted.

Traditionally, a First Sergeant signs for only one item on a company's property book: the Guidon. Bravo Company isn't traditional anymore. We're one of the few units where the 1SG signs for two items: the Guidon and the Company Bastard Sword. For us, the sword is not décor; it's identity. It is who we are when things get hard. Buying a bastard sword was easy, but the impact it had on our culture was enormous.

The doubts that once held me back became the empathy that pushed me forward. The weaknesses I carried became the strengths I needed to steady an entire company. When you're lost, the lessons you learn when fighting your way back will prepare you to lead others home in the future.

The call from the Sergeant Major wasn't just a return to a company; it was a reminder to us that our leadership journey never ends. Sometimes it loops back on itself just to make sure you know how far you've come.

Throughout my career, I've accumulated wins, losses, and more than a few humorous moments that have shaped me, for better and for worse, into the leader I am today. I hope this book provides the azimuth a new organizational leader needs as they begin their own journey.

If you have ever wondered, "Am I really ready for this new position?" Then this book is for you.

Contents

Chapter One

Introduction

Why leadership matters now more than ever.

"Ranks and titles are temporary, but the way you treat people lasts forever."
— Anonymous

Bad leaders suck!

We've all served under, or survived, leaders who prove that rank and position are impressive accessories, but lousy substitutes for real leadership. A leader's legacy isn't measured by the rank or position they hold; those come with the job. It's measured by their actions, the example they set, and how they treated their people when no one was watching. Sure, we can complain about terrible leaders for days, trading stories like MRE snacks at a field exercise. Long after people forget your rank and stop using your title, they'll remember your conduct, your example, and how you treated them. Which begs the question we rarely ask ourselves:

What if I'm the bad leader in someone else's story?

I was fortunate enough to learn that lesson the hard way.

Years after my first deployment, life handed me one of those full-circle moments, a chance to see who I *really* was long before I knew any better. While making rounds to visit some ranges during a drill weekend, I visited the mortar live-fire range. Mortar ranges are always an exhilarating experience. To see, hear, and feel the mortar tubes in action, launching high-angle mortars to precise targets, is truly an impressive experience. Looking at one of the mortar teams, I noticed a familiar face. It was a Soldier who had served under me back when I was a young, eager team leader trying to make my mark. I remembered him as a good kid back then. We hadn't seen each other for many years, and he was now a Staff Sergeant, leading his section of mortarmen. I was genuinely excited to hear about how he had been after we all went our separate ways after that deployment.

I learned after a few minutes of catching up that I was the bad leader in his story. He was candid in our conversation. My poor leadership left a lasting impression on him. One that I was not proud of.

He remembered my attempt at leadership, which was more imitation than intention. What I thought was "toughening Soldiers up" was, in his memory, nothing more than constant punishment disguised as physical fitness. He asked if I remembered putting him through the wringer day after day. I honestly barely remembered any specifics. What I remembered was mimicking what I had experienced as a young private: a cycle of small, seemingly harmless "gut checks" that, in reality, were nothing more than ritualized suffering with no real purpose. In truth, it was a mask for me to hide behind, covering up my incompetence. Worst of all, he was now emulating how I had treated him. He became a terrible leader in other soldiers' stories, and I was the root cause of that. I apologized to him for my poor judgement, but it fell on deaf ears; to him, the only inspiration I gave him was negative.

It was a humbling moment for me.

I had to accept the truth that I had been precisely the type of leader I preached against. Not malicious, not intentionally cruel, but misguided. And when your leading teams, misguided leadership can still leave scars. It isn't easy to know how your actions impact the future, unless you are privileged enough to experience an interaction like the one I had with that young Staff Sergeant. It is very easy not to be overly concerned about the consequences of your actions, especially in the present. However, when you stay with an organization long enough, your future may meet your past self. You will notice the lasting impact you have had on the people you work with. Hopefully, yours will be more positive than what I experienced that day.

That encounter didn't just remind me of who I was; it helped me to reshape who I needed to become. It forced me to confront the truth that leadership isn't a title you get when you're promoted; it's a responsibility you grow toward, and growth takes time. In the end, the two things that shaped me into the leader I became were simple: time and mistakes... and I got more than my fair share of both. Not the catastrophic mistakes you hear about in the latest office gossip, but the subtle, quiet missteps that accumulate over years: the conversations I should have had, the Soldiers I failed to understand, the moments where ego spoke louder than empathy. Every one of those missteps left a mark, and every mark carried a lesson. As a leader, you need to cultivate self-awareness to recognize your mistakes and to have the humility to admit your failures, then get back on the right track.

With time, I learned to stop mimicking the loudest examples and start finding my way to lead. Real leadership is about owning the impact of your actions. The Soldiers I influenced, whether positively or negatively, were mirrors reflecting the quality of my leadership. And sometimes, that reflection was hard to look at. Over time, I learned to grow and became the mentor I once needed as a junior leader.

Growth rarely happens in comfort. It happens when your past confronts your present and demands something better from your future. To get there, you must face your failures and learn from every experience, especially the ones you'd rather forget.

Self-awareness is easy to discuss but brutally hard to put into practice. Nobody wants to sit down and take an inventory of how badly they've screwed up as a leader. We all prefer to hear about how exceptional we are. And let's be honest, people often hand out praise to leaders who haven't earned it, reinforcing blind spots instead of challenging them. I have seen this and, like many others, have been guilty of perpetuating the tradition of misguiding Soldiers about their performance. Authentic leadership means taking action and starting tough conversations about poor performance. It means offering a clear azimuth that helps people realign, grow, and become better humans, not just better Soldiers.

The chance encounter I had with that Staff Sergeant was a poignant reminder of how every leader can have an impact, even if it may not always be positive.

So why does leadership matter more now than ever? Because people are starving for it. Not authority, not managers, but leaders. **Real ones!** Someone who listens, supports growth, sets clear goals, and truly cares about their team. Excellent leadership is not as common as we think, not because people don't want to lead well, but because it requires work, modesty, and consistency. Not all assigned leaders have those attributes. Some organizations fail to recognize and reward these qualities. Instead, we commonly promote statistical metrics and hope leadership magically happens. Or worse, organizations often reward outstanding leaders with more work, sometimes leading to burnout or failure. This can cause overworked high-performing leaders, to where they leave your organization, effectively killing retention.

Too often, leaders inflict "performance punishment" on their most reliable people simply for being dependable. High performers get overloaded with more work, tighter deadlines, and higher expectations—because managers know they'll deliver—while underperformers receive lighter loads, since it's easier to avoid confronting their shortcomings. It may sound ridiculous, yet this pattern is distressingly common in many organizations.

The second-, third-, and fourth-order effects are even more damaging. When teams rely solely on the same "easy-button" personnel to handle the hardest tasks, development stalls. Successors go untrained and under-prepared. Eventually, the organization wakes up to a shallow bench: no one qualified in the succession pipeline, key knowledge concentrated in a few overburdened individuals, and rapid vulnerability when those stars inevitably burn out, disengage, or depart.

We're operating in a world full of distractions, demands, staff shortages, broken processes, shifting priorities, and "do more with less" expectations. Soldiers are carrying heavier loads, both mentally and physically, as well as emotionally and geographically. The Army is evolving faster than ever, and the price of bad leadership has never been higher. A Soldier can survive a bad day, but they suffer needlessly under a terrible leader.

So, let's do what we can to correct our azimuth and point our compass in the right direction, even if the path is uncomfortable, uphill, or forces us to confront things we'd rather avoid. That's what this book is: a **"panic azimuth"** for leaders stepping into senior roles, a reference you can grab when everything feels chaotic, uncertain, or overwhelming.

These pages are lessons I learned the hard way, over years of trial and error, and the experiences one can only earn under pressure, forged in time. I hope you use them to shape who you are as a leader, who you want to become, and ultimately how those you lead will remember you.

Most of this book is grounded in my experience within the Army National Guard, as an Infantry First Sergeant and S3 Operations supervisor, simply because those were the most recent senior leadership positions I held before deciding to retire from the Army. That context matters, but don't make the mistake of thinking these lessons only apply to the Guard. Nothing could be further from the truth.

The principles, lessons, and examples throughout this book are universal. Leadership is leadership, regardless of component, rank, or uniform. Whether you're serving in the National Guard, Active Duty, Reserves, or leading in a civilian organization, the fundamentals remain the same. These lessons apply just as much to a company First Sergeant or Commander as they do to a Platoon Sergeant, Team Leader, or civilian manager.

People still need direction. Teams still experience friction. Decisions still carry consequences. And leaders are still judged by their actions, not their intentions. No matter the environment, effective leadership is about trust, discipline, accountability, and investing in your people and in yourself.

If you can lead Soldiers, you can lead in any formation. And if you understand these principles, you can apply them anywhere life puts you in charge.

Who the Hell Is This Guy?

Before we go any further, it is only fair that I explain who I am and the experiences that shaped the perspective behind this book.

First, I am a Soldier, a warfighter, and a combat leader. For over two decades, I have led Soldiers in the most demanding environments our nation has faced. My career has not been defined by rank or assignment, but by responsibility. The responsibility to close with the enemy, to make decisions under fire, and to ensure the men and women entrusted to me received the leadership they deserved and the best possible chance of coming home. My leadership journey spans over 26 years in the Army, Army Reserve, and Army National Guard.

I enlisted in the United States Army Infantry in August 2000, during what was considered a period of relative calm. Assigned to the 5th Battalion, 20th Infantry Regiment (5-20 IN), stationed in the beautiful Pacific Northwest, at what is now called Joint Base Lewis-McChord (JBLM). We trained extensively in close-quarters urban combat: room clearing, instinctive shooting, and the disciplined aggression required when the fight is measured in feet rather than miles. We trained hard, unaware how soon those skills would be tested.

September 11, 2001, ended the illusion of peacetime.

I never deployed with 5-20 IN since my active-duty service concluded in 2003, after which I transitioned briefly into civilian life. I was then assigned to the Inactive Ready Reserve (IRR), an Army Reserve component. That IRR break did not last long. After only two years, I was recalled and plunged back into service. From that point forward, I led Soldiers through repeated deployments across multiple components of the Army. I deployed to Iraq in 2005–2006 with the Wisconsin Army National Guard's 32nd Brigade Combat Team. I returned to Iraq from 2008 to 2009 with the Washington Army National Guard's 81st Brigade Combat Team. In those years, leadership lessons were forged in the fires of war.

The most intense chapter of my service came in 2012–2013, when I served as a combat advisor embedded with Afghan Security Forces. That deployment was the most kinetic of my career, and it remains the one I speak about the least.

From 2021 to 2022, I served as a combat advisor to the Armed Forces of Ukraine as they defended their nation against a near-peer adversary. Watching that conflict unfold reinforced a truth I had learned years earlier: while technology evolves and weapons change, the fundamentals of war do not. Discipline, trust, preparation, and the human domain remain decisive. It was also the first time in my career that I saw tangible results of my efforts at a national level, though I played only a small part.

I advanced through the Infantry the traditional way: Rifleman, Automatic Rifleman, Team Leader, Squad Leader, Platoon Sergeant, and now serve as First Sergeant of Broadsword Company, 1-161 Infantry, Washington Army National Guard. I led Soldiers directly, whether during training cycles, operational planning, or on the line where leadership matters most. I have also served as a U.S. Army instructor, preparing future leaders by pairing tactical skill development with academic lessons.

I entered the Active Guard Reserve (AGR) program in 2013 as a full-time instructor. In 2017, I transitioned to Bravo Company as the AGR Readiness NCO while also serving as a Platoon Sergeant, balancing the administrative and tactical responsibilities that come with both roles. In 2020, I was promoted to First Sergeant in that same company. Since then, I have served as an Infantry Company First Sergeant across four companies—one of which I had the privilege of leading twice.

At 43 years old and serving as a First Sergeant, I attended and graduated Ranger School with Class 3-23, one of the most demanding leadership crucibles in the Army. The course tests physical endurance, mental toughness, and small-unit tactics through relentless sleep deprivation, ruck marches, patrols, and peer evaluations across mountains, swamps, and urban environments. I did not pass on my first attempt; I was recycled in Mountain Phase, twice. A hell I wish on no one.

I am a graduate of the U.S. Army Sergeants Major Academy, a milestone that places me among the Army's most senior enlisted leaders in terms of military education. Many of the Sergeants Major I served alongside were my peers, fellow First Sergeants, senior advisors, and combat leaders who shared the same experiences, responsibilities, and standards. Because of structural limitations within the National Guard AGR system, specifically constrained senior enlisted billets and controlled-grade allocations, I will never formally wear the rank of Sergeant Major. I remain at peace with that outcome.

This book is not written from a distance. It does not come from a staff desk, an academic model, or unearned hindsight. It is written by someone who has stood in the breach as a warfighter, made life-and-death decisions as a combat leader, and carried the enduring responsibility of being an NCO entrusted with the lives, readiness, and morale of others.

What Is a Panic Azimuth?

If you're not from a military background, the title *Panic Azimuth* might sound cryptic. Let me explain.

In land navigation training in the Army, Soldiers learn to move across rugged, unforgiving terrain using only a map, protractor, and compass. No GPS, no cell phone, no trail markers. You plot your course, shoot azimuths (bearings from north), count your paces, and navigate point to point, often at night or in dense woods where one wrong turn can leave you completely disoriented.

Before heading out, the instructors give a safety briefing. Part of that brief is the **panic azimuth**, a pre-planned emergency bearing you memorize or keep in your pocket. If you get hopelessly lost, low on water, or injured, you stop trying to find your next point. Instead, you **shoot the panic azimuth**, set your compass to that fixed direction, and walk it straight until you hit a known safe feature: usually a major road or patrol route where search teams are actively looking for you. It's your lifeline, your reset button. You don't second-guess it; you trust it and move on.

The term "panic" doesn't mean running blindly; it means when fear, fatigue, or confusion threatens to take over. The azimuth is the deliberate choice to stop wandering in circles and head toward safety with purpose.

In this book, *Panic Azimuth* is that same concept applied to leadership. When you're overwhelmed in a new senior role, doubts creeping in, the mission feels chaotic, decisions are piling up, or you're questioning whether you're the right person for the seat, you don't freeze or flail. You stop, orient yourself, drink some water, listen to your surroundings, reset, shoot your azimuth, and head toward true north. You are not alone, nor the first to experience this.

It's not about avoiding panic; it's about having a pre-planned direction to follow when panic arrives. That's the azimuth this book provides: a clear, reliable bearing to get you moving forward again, even when the map feels useless and the terrain is unforgiving.

Chapter Two

The Foundation

Core Values of a Leader

> *"Read the NCO Creed every now and then, ask yourself, are you doing those things?"*

The Army gives us a doctrinal blueprint for leadership in ADP 6-22: *Army Leadership and the Profession* ADP 6-22[1]. It's a solid resource, clear, structured, and packed with definitions of what leadership is and how the Army expects leaders to practice it.

But let's be honest: The ADP 6-22 is not exactly the type of book you curl up with for fun. It reads like...well, a regulation. Necessary, but not exactly action-packed or memorable. You can memorize the Army's definition of leadership: *"Leadership is the activity of influencing people by providing purpose, direction, and motivation to accomplish the mission and improve the organization,"* but memorizing doctrine doesn't automatically translate into living it or putting it into practice on the front lines.

This chapter is about laying the foundation and digging deeper into the core values of a leader. What the regulation doesn't give you is the human side of leadership. It doesn't explain what "providing purpose" looks like at 0200 when morale is tanking. This doesn't describe the anxiety related to the decisions you make that affect soldiers' lives. It does not show the messy, gritty realities, the part where people, emotions, and consequences collide. And that's where leaders can struggle. Doctrine explains *what* leadership is. Experience teaches you *how to* apply leadership effectively.

After years of hearing the Army's definition of leadership and seeing it done both well and poorly, it's worth unpacking what "purpose, direction, and motivation" really look like in practice.

Purpose is the foundation of any organization. It defines why the unit exists and what it is ultimately meant to accomplish. For an infantry company, that purpose can be stated plainly: to close with and destroy the enemy of our nation. Clear purpose gives meaning to the mission and aligns every action toward a common end state.

Direction is how the organization sharpens itself to fulfill that purpose. It is the plan, the training focus, and the standards that guide the unit toward excellence. Direction turns intent into action, it ensures that time, resources, and energy are applied in ways that make the unit more capable and more lethal.

Motivation is the most complex of the three. It is influenced by many factors: conditions, leadership, trust, and individual mindset. Unlike purpose and direction, it cannot simply be assigned. However, leaders can influence it by creating the conditions where motivation is more likely to emerge and be sustained. When leaders demonstrate genuine commitment and belief in the unit's purpose, that influence shapes the organizational climate. Over time, that presence can become contagious, and it often provides the spark a team needs to push forward and perform at its best.

Chip and Dan Heath's book, *Made to Stick* Heath[2] argues that ideas gain meaning, become memorable, and turn into action when they are anchored in clarity, emotion, and story. Leadership is no different. ADP 6-22 provides the framework, but it's lived experiences, failures included, that make those principles actually *stick*. Throughout this book, I will do my best to link lessons to some stories and insights I have gained throughout my tenure as a senior leader: not just reciting the words of ADP 6-22 but connecting its principles to genuine emotions and experiences. The values you don't just memorize but embody. My hope is that by the end of this book, you'll be better equipped to provide purpose, direction, and motivation to those you lead.

The quote, "Read the NCO Creed now and then, ask yourself, are you doing those things?" is something I said to every new NCO during their initial counseling. That counseling always comes with a nicely framed copy of the NCO Creed. They should read it periodically and honestly question if they're living those words. I don't expect anyone to memorize it—it is 289 words long. I can barely remember to bring my lunch to work, let alone flawlessly recite a creed I once memorized over twenty years ago back at PLDC (an acronym from a bygone era). Still, the creed remains an outstanding tool for a quick leadership tune-up, a way to recalibrate before you drift too far off course.

There have been plenty of times when I've read the NCO creed and thought, *"Dude... you are not doing many of these things well right now."* It is humbling, but it's necessary. The NCO Creed is probably one of the best azimuth checks you can get; it is where I based mine on. What matters comes next. I do everything I can to **take action** instead of just acknowledging my failures and walking away from the responsibility to fix them. Putting ideas into action is challenging, time-consuming, and sometimes frustrating, but the benefits far outweigh the costs.

Remember, you're not taking action to do these things for yourself. You are the senior leader; you owe it to those young Soldiers or employees you work **for**—yes, *for*, not "over." Your primary customer is the newest, lowest-ranking, youngest person in your formation or organization. That's who you should be focused on. That's who you should try to impress. Not your boss. Not higher headquarters. Not the people who already have power. Your people are the mission. They are the future leaders. Impress the hell out of them with what real leadership looks like, because the ones you inspire now are the ones who'll carry the fight when you're gone.

Stop obsessing over your next promotion. That takes care of itself if you apply these principles written throughout this book. A positive side effect of genuinely investing in and caring about your team is that their results become impossible for higher headquarters to ignore. When your team performs, when your unit functions well, your higher leadership notices, and that reflection lands squarely on you. Because you generated tangible results through outstanding leadership.

Understanding What Makes a Leader

Before we delve deeper into leadership, it helps to strip away the jargon and examine what the Army is *actually* referring to when it defines a leader. ADP 6-22 breaks leadership into two simple pieces: who you are and what you do. Simple on paper, surprisingly easy to overcomplicate in real life.

What follows is my attempt to translate the Army's version into something more relatable for both upcoming leaders and senior leaders who've been in the fight long enough to know that doctrine doesn't always match reality.

Core Leader Attributes—Who You Are

Attributes are the things built inside you, the stuff that drives how you think, act, and respond when the heat gets turned up. These aren't skills you check off on a course roster; they're the qualities that shape your decisions when it really matters.

The Army groups these attributes into three buckets:

• **Character:** This is your moral compass, the stuff that guides you when nobody's watching. It's the integrity you protect, the values you refuse to compromise, and the standards you uphold even when it would be easier to look the other way. You don't build character in a classroom. It's cultivated through your screw-ups, your victories, the people who mentored you, and the moments life kicked you in the teeth and whispered, *"Do better."*

• **Presence:** This people see long before they hear you speak. It's your confidence (real or temporarily rented), your physical bearing, and how you carry yourself when things get chaotic and everyone else is losing their minds. Presence can't be fast-tracked or faked for long. It takes miles, mistakes, and time under tension to develop. Soldiers instantly recognize when a leader has truly earned their presence and when it is fake.

• **Intellect:** This is your ability to think clearly, solve actual problems, make smart decisions, and stay mentally agile when the plan catches on fire. It is also how well you understand people, not just tasks, checklists, or doctrine. Intellect grows only if you keep learning, keep asking questions, and stay current with new ideas and better methods. Leaders who stop learning become the leaders others stop following. Great news! If you are reading this book, you are taking steps towards learning, so fantastic work!

Strong attributes give a leader real depth. They are what make you trustworthy and stable when that situation tests your resolve. These qualities are what your subordinates expect from you and what your supervisors rely on you to deliver, every single day, including when you are at home.

When the Army writes about these wonderful leadership attributes, it reads like you already possess them, as if you woke up one day with a flawless character, unshakeable presence, and an Einstein-level intellect. However, it's good for leaders to know the reality here: you don't just "arrive" at these qualities. You **build** them.

Your brain does not receive these attributes like software downloads. They're earned through experience. The Army can describe what a leader *should* be, but only real life teaches you how to become one. The best way to develop these characteristics is to seek new opportunities that are uncomfortable or challenging.

Remember that comfort equals stagnation. So, get dirty, test your limits, find leadership positions that are uncomfortable and challenging.

Three additional attributes I'd include are patience, humility, and fortitude. Doctrine provides the framework, but real leadership emerges in the spaces it doesn't explicitly address, the moments that demand character beyond what's written.

• **Patience:** This keeps you from losing your mind when a private asks, "Hey, First Sergeant, have you seen my weapon?" A question no private should ask, ever. It's what stops you from reacting emotionally when a situation needs a steady mind instead of a sharp tongue. Patience isn't passive; it's controlled strength. It will test your emotional regulation to the limit.

• **Humility:** This is the anchor that keeps you grounded when rank, authority, or success tries to inflate your ego. It's admitting when you don't know something, owning it when you screw up, and giving credit away even when you could just as easily keep it. Humility makes you teachable, approachable, and human. To Soldiers, this matters way more than any rank on your uniform.

The fastest way to stop learning is to believe you already know everything. If you think you've got it all figured out, that's precisely when you need to use your humility, listen, and let another perspective in. It might challenge you. It might even dismantle what you thought you knew. However, that's how leaders grow, by choosing humility over what you think you already know.

• **Fortitude:** This is the quiet toughness that shows up when the mission gets ugly, the hours get long, or the decisions get heavy. It's the inner grit that lets you stand firm when everyone is looking at you for answers. Fortitude isn't about being unbreakable; it's about being able to bend without quitting.

These additional attributes don't show up on an evaluation report or a checklist, but Soldiers notice them. They feel them. Over time, these "extra" characteristics often end up defining a leader far more than a paragraph in doctrine ever will.

Core Leader Competencies—What You Do

Attributes are who you are on the inside; competencies are the actions you put into the world. These are the things the Army expects every leader to **do,** no matter their rank, job, or component. These are the tangible deliverables senior leaders are expected to produce.

The Army breaks them down into three categories:

• **Leads:** This is where you actually *influence humans*, real people with emotions, opinions, and at least one Platoon Sergeant who swears he "totally read the Operations Order." You give purpose, direction, and influence motivation, even when the mission changes three times before lunch. You communicate clearly (or at least try to), set the example, and build trust one action at a time, even when you're running on caffeine and optimism.

• **Develops:** This is the part where you become part leader, part counselor, part-time parent. You invest in people because someone once invested in you. Work on improving yourself, even if it means admitting you don't have all the answers (spoiler: none of us do). You build a climate where people feel safe owning mistakes and learning from them. You coach, mentor, and help shape the profession for the next generation, knowing full well they'll someday replace you, probably with someone who is younger, faster, smarter, and better looking.

• **Achieves:** The Army, and any high-performing organization, demands results, not excuses. You execute, adapt, and deliver, sometimes according to plan, sometimes through sheer grit. Sometimes by cobbling it together with zip ties, duct tape, WD-40, and an NCO's classic "trust me, it'll work." You turn doctrine and concepts into reality, keep the mission moving despite friction, weather, or every unforeseen curveball. You get it done to standard, on time, often with no one ever knowing how many disasters you quietly averted along the way.

I would only add one more competency to this list:

• **Audacity:** The courage to make hard calls when the path isn't clear. The willingness to stand up, take ownership, and challenge the status quo, even when it's uncomfortable, unpopular, or risky. Audacity isn't recklessness; it's the guts to act decisively when inaction would jeopardize your Soldiers, the mission, or your integrity. It's the spark that turns good leaders into great ones.

Together, these competencies make leadership something you do, not just something you talk about. They turn all the values, ideas, and good intentions into real actions, especially on the days when things go wrong, people are tired, and nothing is going according to plan. Leadership stops being a concept and becomes the way you show up, make decisions, support your team, and keep the mission. It's not theoretical. It's lived through stress, mistakes, small victories, and every messy human moment in between.

Leadership, according to the Army, comes down to two things: **who you are** and **what you do**. Attributes shape your internal foundation, your character, your presence, and your intellect. These aren't checklist items or classroom lessons; they're created the hard way through messy experiences and the moments that force you to grow. The other add-on attributes, patience, humility, and fortitude, also play a significant role, even if they are not included in doctrine. Soldiers notice them, rely on them, and expect them to be there.

Competencies are the outward actions of leadership, **how you influence, develop, and accomplish the mission**. Leading means guiding actual humans, even those who definitely did not read the operations order. Developing means investing in people, building a healthy climate, and staying teachable yourself. Achieving means executing and adapting, delivering results even when friction, chaos, or the weather makes it interesting.

Together, attributes and competencies turn leadership from a buzzword into a lived reality. Not something you recite, but something you perform, especially when things get hard, plans fall apart, and people are counting on you. Ultimately, leadership is built in the real world. These lessons have to be lived; there is no better way. Leaders cannot shield their Soldiers from the hard parts or failures of the journey; they need to experience it themselves. Your role is to guide them, provide the tools, and give them a "panic azimuth" to point the way when things get messy.

Leadership is a privilege, and trust is the currency that sustains it. Every single day, you are either earning that trust or quietly eroding it. The NCO Creed isn't just something to recite at a ceremony; it's a standard your Soldiers measure you against, whether or not you realize it. And eventually, that reality gets documented.

That's where evaluations come in.

Evaluations are the formal record of your leadership, how well you developed others, enforced standards, and carried the weight of your role. They translate day-to-day leadership into long-term impact, shaping careers, opportunities, and futures long after you've moved on to your next assignment.

Evaluations

Now, let's talk about every senior leader's favorite thing in the entire Army: **Evaluations**. *Yay!!* Go ahead, try to contain your excitement.

If you've ever watched a room full of NCOs suddenly develop the thousand-yard stare, just say the words "NCOERs" or "NCOER support form." It's like summoning a collective mass of spiritual exhaustion. Evaluations are the dental cleaning of military leadership: everyone knows they're necessary, nobody wakes up excited to do them, and if you ignore them long enough, everything decays.

I have seen too many leaders treat them like a chore to complete instead of a responsibility to develop people. Some leaders inflate their Soldier's accomplishments to avoid tough conversations. Others hyper-inflate mediocrity. Some write evaluations as if they're building a Marvel superhero, while others fill them out as if they're completing a rental car form.

That's exactly why this belongs squarely in Foundations. Leadership goes way beyond philosophy or battlefield tactics; its real bedrock is the systems and mechanisms that carry it forward across the entire force. Evaluations give senior leaders arguably the single most powerful lever to shape culture, develop talent, and build the next echelon. Yet they're also the most misused (or just flat-out misunderstood), routinely placing unqualified leaders in roles they have no business holding.

To put it bluntly, we suck at evaluations and leveraging them to truly develop leaders.

Evaluations aren't about making someone feel warm and fuzzy or checking a box before the suspense date hits. They're about telling the truth and charting a developmental path. They give a Soldier the professional mirror they need, even when they don't want to investigate it. And here's the part people hate to admit: it's okay to need improvement. That's how development actually happens. We have to stop pretending that checking the "needs improvement" block ruins careers. In reality, refusing to use it is what stunts growth and professional development.

If you look back on your own career, you'll probably find moments where a "needs improvement" block would have helped you. If you honestly believe otherwise, then you're lying to yourself, and that's a sign of poor self-awareness and a lack of humility, not superior performance.

So yeah... evaluations...the thing everyone hates talking about, but every good leader needs to master.

The Army uses the Army Evaluation Entry System (EES). It is a secure, web-based platform managed by the U.S. Army Human Resources Command (HRC) for creating, processing, and submitting performance evaluations. It handles Officer Evaluation Reports (OERs) for commissioned officers and Non-Commissioned

Officer Evaluation Reports (NCOERs) for enlisted leaders, such as sergeants and above. These reports evaluate a soldier's performance, leadership, and potential, driving promotions, assignments, and career progression, much like a high-stakes corporate review.

To a non-military audience, EES functions like a collaborative online HR tool with built-in rules and safeguards. Users log in securely using a military Common Access Card (CAC), similar to a government-issued digital ID. The process typically begins with a support form, where the rated soldier documents accomplishments and goals. Support forms are useful, but not absolutely necessary. The rater (direct supervisor) then completes detailed sections on attributes like character, competence, and leadership, while the senior rater provides an independent assessment of promotion potential and compares the soldier to peers using enforced rating profiles to prevent inflation. Everyone signs digitally in sequence, beginning with the rater, senior rater, then Soldier, in that order. The system validates for errors, enforces Army regulations, and allows the senior rater to submit the completed report electronically to headquarters. If issues arise, it's returned for fixes; once approved, it updates the soldier's official record, streamlining what was once a paper-heavy process into a more efficient, trackable digital workflow.

There are a ton of potential issues that can arise during the evaluation process, such as poorly written or misspelled bullet comments, raters improperly predicting future potential, or missing data like counseling dates and fitness information. However, one of the primary obstacles to timely processing is getting the required signatures. While the digital signature requirement cannot be bypassed, the number of signatures can be minimized through proper rating chain configuration and procedural allowances.

I accidentally influenced the organization's echelons above my own because I cared about something most people avoid. I set one simple goal for my company: *zero* NCOER delinquencies. Not "better than last year." Not "Let's try harder." Zero. And I didn't just announce it; I built a system to make it happen. Some people didn't like my method, and that's fine. Leadership isn't a popularity contest. However, you need to understand the environment in which I worked. I was in a National Guard unit. I saw my NCOs and Soldiers one weekend a month. That's it. Twelve, sometimes less, cracks a year at getting it right. I achieved my goals and continue to believe that B-Co 1-161 is the sole infantry company in the entire Army to reach and uphold that accomplishment. Yeah, that's a hell of a claim, but prove me wrong. I'd love to be corrected. If another company steps up, great; it means more senior leaders are finally delivering fair, on-time ratings to every NCO, as we should be.

How did I get to zero delinquent NCOERs? Brace yourself—this one's controversial. I removed two signature requirements. First, my company commander, an O-3, doesn't need a reviewer, which means he serves as the senior rater for all my NCOs in the entire company. Second, if the rated NCO can't sign when needed, they are simply marked not available for signature. No excuses, no delays. Love it or hate it, the results speak for themselves: zero delinquent NCOERs. If a Soldier disagrees with their rating, they may appeal in accordance with Army policy. This method allows me, as a leader, to track, manage, and review every NCOER in the unit. The commander has designated me as a profile delegate. I can submit NCOERs to HQDA or remove signatures on the commander's behalf, ensuring that nothing stalls and every evaluation proceeds on time.

AR 623–3[3] explicitly allows this. The regulation states that when a rated Soldier is unavailable, the rater annotates the report so that it can proceed without delay. This preserves the integrity of the evaluation system and protects the Soldier's promotion eligibility. In a National Guard environment, where you only see your Soldiers one weekend a month, waiting indefinitely for a signature isn't feasible. By marking the rated NCOs as not available for signature, when necessary, I ensured full compliance with AR 623–3, eliminated delinquent NCOERs, and prevented any Soldier from being unfairly penalized by a promotion board.

The impact of having no current evaluations is almost as damaging as showing up to a promotion board with a recent DUI. From the board's perspective, how can they assess someone who has no current evaluations?

Easy, negatively.

This may not be the case for every promotion board; I can only speak from my experience sitting on past boards in my organization. Maybe your organization has a more refined or disciplined system. If so, that's outstanding. But regardless of how any board operates, the truth remains the same: when a Soldier has no evaluations; it is a terrible way to select the future leaders of an organization.

Here's another debatable process I follow. Anytime I have to wait on another unit outside my organization to complete an evaluation, I'm almost guaranteed to be let down. When I identify a delinquent NCOER for an incoming Soldier from another unit, I give the outside unit one chance—a hard deadline. Once that time passes, which it inevitably does, I take ownership. That Soldier and I have a discussion about their accomplishments in the previous unit, I gave them the benefit of the doubt, and I complete the evaluation myself.

I apply Jocko Willink's Extreme Ownership[4] approach, I take responsibility for the issue, avoid shifting blame, and shield Soldiers from being held accountable for failures outside of their control.

Controversial? Possibly. Effective? Undeniably. And in the world of leadership, sometimes you have to make the hard call to get the right results. This system worked. That is how I was able to influence a few organizations well above my little company level. Organizations saw that it worked and applied those methods to help reduce their delinquency rates. I would argue that this solution is not a sustainable answer, it's simply a method to get your delinquent NCOERs cleared.

Evaluations of your Soldiers are your responsibility as a leader; no shortcuts, no excuses. If I had a magic wand and were king of the Army, I'd make an NCOER delinquency report a mandatory part of every senior leader promotion board packet. That would quickly teach leaders some hard consequences of letting their evaluations slip. Ultimately, fixing delinquent elevations will be in the best interest of the Soldier, the only one to suffer from leadership failing to evaluate them fairly—and on time.

Evaluations aren't about paperwork, signatures, or dodging suspense dates; they're about stewardship. They're about taking responsibility for the careers, futures, and opportunities of the Soldiers entrusted to you. My methods weren't always popular, nor were they conventional, but they worked because they were founded on a single core belief: leaders must provide their people with honest and timely evaluations.

What I learned, sometimes the hard way, is that good leaders don't let the system happen to their Soldiers. They shape the system to protect their Soldiers. They find ways to make the process work, even in the chaos of a one-weekend-a-month National Guard schedule. They take ownership when others won't. They tell the truth when it's easier to avoid it. They do the hard right instead of the easy wrong.

If you take nothing else from this section, take this:

Evaluations are one of the most powerful tools you have to influence, develop, and advocate for your Soldiers. Treat them like it.

Your legacy as a leader won't be measured by how many NCOERs you completed; it will be measured by how many careers you shaped because you cared enough to do them right. And sometimes, leadership really is that simple: caring enough to take ownership, caring enough to do the hard things, and caring enough to ensure every Soldier receives the evaluation they deserve.

That's how you build trust. That's how you build readiness. And that's how you build leaders.

Take action, own the problem, and fix it!

Wrapping It Up

At its core, leadership is both simple and demanding: it's about who you are, what you actually do, and the real impact you have on the people you lead. This chapter was all about laying the foundation. Being a good leader isn't memorizing ADP 6-22, reciting the NCO Creed word-for-word, or checking boxes on some eval form. It's about living the values, showing the attributes, and executing the competencies in ways that actually inspire trust, get people moving, and build real resilience in the team. It's about stepping up and doing the hard thing when it's needed most—not when it's convenient.

Leadership isn't built from memorizing doctrine or reciting creeds; it's built from what you do when no one is watching and when everything is falling apart at the same time. ADP 6-22 gives us the framework, but experience gives it meaning. The NCO Creed gives us the standard, but honest reflection tells us whether we're actually living it.

Attributes shape who you are. Competencies define what you do. Systems like evaluations reveal whether your leadership truly affects others. Together, they form a simple truth: leadership is stewardship. It's the responsibility to develop people, protect their futures, and leave the organization stronger than you found it.

Every day is an azimuth check. Ask yourself if your actions match your values, if your decisions serve your Soldiers, and if you're taking ownership when things get hard. Leadership isn't about being perfect; it's about choosing action over comfort and responsibility over convenience.

And that's exactly why evaluations belong right here in Foundations. They're the single most powerful tool senior leaders have to shape culture, grow talent, and build the next group of leaders. The problem is, we're terrible at them, or we just don't get them. Too many people treat them like a chore, inflate ratings to dodge hard talks, or let delinquencies slide. But we can't keep doing that. Honest, on-time evaluations are how you hold up the mirror, chart a real path forward, and make sure no Soldier's career gets quietly wrecked by inaction.

Your legacy? It will not be how many NCOERs you cranked out or how shiny your bullets looked. It's going to be how many Soldiers you refused to let the system screw over—how many careers you protected, how many junior leaders you helped grow, and how many privates saw what real leadership actually looks like because you gave a damn.

So yeah... read the NCO Creed now and then. Then ask yourself straight up: Am I actually living this? And if the answer is no, adjust course and get back to work.

Focus on impressing the newest, lowest-ranking, youngest person in your formation. They're not just "your people"—they're your mission. They're the future. Invest in them, tell them the truth, fight for their opportunities, and show them through your actions what leadership really means.

Do the work. Live the values. Own the results. Provide clear purpose, direction, and create the conditions for motivation to thrive—consistently.

That's the foundation for building trust, forging actual leaders, and creating high-performing teams.

Chapter Three

Building Trust

Difficult to Build, but Effortless to Lose.

> *"Never underestimate the power of a formation."*

The First Formation: Where Trust Begins

In the Army, especially in the National Guard, the first formation is the absolute best time to set the tone for the entire drill. It's your opening statement. It's the moment you give the azimuth and trajectory for the entire week or weekend, intentionally or not. And the leaders who get this right understand that formation isn't about rattling off tasks or lecturing about what needs to happen; it's also the best opportunity to recognize your people, not requirements.

When you highlight a Soldier for their performance, pin a promotion in front of their peers, or present an award at first formation, you're doing far more than checking a ceremonial box, you're sending a message: **I see you, what you do matters. You earned this moment.** Leaders often fail to realize the significant impact of even the smallest action.

I've seen too many leaders skip their first formations because they think it's unnecessary, inconvenient, or "something the platoon sergeant can handle." While

I'm a huge believer in delegation, some things in our profession are sacred, and formations are one of them.

In the Army, the first formation is a 1SG's **most formidable weapon** for shaping culture. It's where standards are set, people are recognized, energy is generated, and trust begins to build. A leader's energy in that moment is contagious; positive, engaged leadership spreads faster than apathy ever will. When leader's hand that moment away or treat it like a chore, they miss one of the easiest wins in the profession of arms. Like any weapon, it should only be used for good and the protection of your people, not to humiliate them.

There is no better confirmation that you're making a positive impact than seeing a Soldier proudly post their award or promotion online. When they're so proud of what they've accomplished, and how they were recognized, that they share it with the world, you've done it right. That's not luck. That's tangible leadership. That's trust being built in real time.

Trust in a formation starts with competence. You will need to spend time studying drill and ceremony. You don't have to master every movement or command, but you need a solid working understanding. That baseline competence gives you the confidence to control a formation instead of being controlled by it.

Intentionally, I never made my formations perfect. I added just enough showmanship to remind the Soldiers that I was human too, fallible, learning, and not above them. I even developed my style for promotions and award presentations. However, the moment I handed the formation back to the commander, I snapped it right back to formal.

That balance mattered. It showed that standards still existed, that professionalism was non-negotiable, and that flexibility had its time and place, at least in theory. I never actually asked anyone if that was the message they took away from my formations. The intent was simple: to build trust.

And trust, once built, becomes the currency that carries you through challenging missions and chaotic drill weekends. However, trust isn't confined to the formation alone. Once you step into a company-level command team, you are no longer just a leader within your unit; you have entered the realm of the public.

You are a public figure now.

When you step into a company-level command team, responsible for roughly 150 souls, you may not realize it, but you've just entered an **entry-level public figure position**. Your influence doesn't stop at the Company Guidon or the unit footprint; it extends into families, Soldier's civilian careers, future leaders, and the culture that will outlive your time in charge. Do not underestimate how much influence you can have to build your formations!

What you choose to do with that influence is entirely up to you. However, if you understand the social power of your position and the reach it gives you, you suddenly realize you have a platform capable of lifting your company to heights they didn't even know were possible. Influence isn't a perk of the job; it *is* the job. Use it deliberately, use it generously, and your formation will follow you wherever you go.

When you step into this newly found public spotlight, you really only have two options: you can shrink back and try to hide in the shadows, or you can step forward and boldly become the public face of your company. Both choices come with risks, but only one of them honors the responsibility you've been given. I'll let you decide which one is best for your company.

Just understand this: once you're out front in your first public figure position, **professionalism becomes your new body armor**. It's the only protection that never fails. Your words, your bearing, your decisions, your discipline, those are now the things that shield you when scrutiny hits, when rumors swirl, or when people look to you to set the example.

Lead with professionalism, and even the hard days become manageable. Lead without it… and the spotlight will burn you fast.

Controlling the Narrative: Your Company Becomes What You Project

Here comes the fun part: **you choose what the public sees.** In other words, you control the narrative. And the narrative I wanted for Bravo Company was straightforward: **we are dedicated to the mission, and we are professionals, regardless of the circumstances.**

We're not the team that bad-mouths others or throws shade at our peers. We do not tear down; we build up. We set the example. We are the quiet professionals who can be counted on for two things:

1. **We can be trusted** to do whatever it takes to get the job done.

2. **We do not complain** about how hard the mission gets—we tighten our rucks and move.

That was the identity I wanted our Soldiers, our sister companies, and our higher command to associate with Bravo Company: not loud, not flashy, not dramatic, just relentlessly competent, relentlessly professional, and relentlessly dependable.

How do you do it? First, you **speak it into existence;** you set the tone, define the standard, and make it clear what your company represents. Then you stay **consistent.** That means publishing high-quality, well-crafted social media posts, using the platforms your Soldiers actually pay attention to, and pushing out messages that reinforce your identity and values.

This is *not* something you delegate to someone who doesn't share your passion or understand the company image you're trying to build. As the leader, **you control the narrative.** Use your sphere of influence intentionally. Push out the messages you want the public, your Soldiers, their families, your sister units, and higher headquarters to see.

When done right, your information flow becomes a force multiplier. It shapes culture, builds pride, and turns your company from just another unit into a brand Soldiers believe in.

Now, I'm not saying you need to become the next multimillion-follower influencer. What I *am* saying is that you should shape the message, set the tone, and then—**smartly**—delegate the actual social media management to the people who can execute it better than you. That's not passing the buck; that is leveraging your assets. Make no mistake, it is very possible to become the next multi-million follower influencer. If that happens, remember your best protection is your professionalism.

You must still review and approve everything before it goes public. That includes verifying the message, the quality of the photos, and the accuracy of the imagery. The last thing you want is to accidentally post an image of a Soldier from your unit who is egregiously out of regs and becomes the punchline of your own page. A classic example of why you check your posts happened to me during a routine Soldier promotion post. I was reviewing a photo, seconds away from posting it to our public page. When one of my squad leaders noticed something small but significant: the Soldier being promoted had his name tapes switched. Innocent mistake, wrong message I wanted to send.

Because we caught it beforehand, I sent the photo back to the Soldier's Squad Leader and told him to get someone with the skills to fix it. That became his "punishment," not in a disciplinary sense, but as a lesson. His Soldier wasn't in the proper uniform, and he hadn't checked his formation. So he got to help me correct it and protect the company's image.

In the end, the picture was fixed with some digital magic; the post went out clean, and nobody outside the chain ever knew the difference. Now, imagine if we hadn't caught it. It wasn't malicious, but even a minor oversight can chip away at the narrative you're trying to build.

That's the reality of being in a company-level command team: **it does not take much to damage your image, but it takes consistent effort to protect it.**

You do not need to be a social media influencer; you just need to protect the narrative of your organization.

Quick note: This approach only applies within the limits of your organizational policy. All use of social media or public communication must comply with established approval processes and guidance.

The Hard Lessons: Watching a Culture Collapse

How did I learn to build trust and organizational culture? Easy, because I watched a bad organization fall apart firsthand.

I was on deployment with a newly formed organization, details intentionally left vague to protect the narrative of others, when I witnessed the rapid unraveling of discipline and good order within an organization. It did not happen overnight. It happened through small decisions, ignored warnings, and a culture that slowly shifted from "almost acceptable" to "completely out of control."

Alcohol was the one common denominator that ran through nearly every disciplinary issue, incident, and leadership challenge we encountered. At first, the problems seemed minor, nothing that raised immediate red flags. But the situation deteriorated rapidly once the command team introduced a policy to allow alcohol to be stored in Soldier's living areas under the guise of "big boy rules."

In theory, it sounded reasonable: treat junior and senior leaders like adults, trust them to self-regulate, and avoid micromanaging off-duty behavior. In practice, it was a disaster. The organization lacked the maturity to handle unrestricted access to alcohol. Standards eroded, accountability vanished, and violations drew little more than slap-on-the- wrist consequences that signaled tolerance rather than correction. What began as minor infractions escalated into serious incidents that eroded unit cohesion and trust.

The hard lesson hit home quickly: when you have junior enlisted Soldiers, junior officers, and first-time deployers, there is no such thing as "big boy rules." Maturity isn't granted by policy; it's built through deliberate leadership, clear boundaries, consistent accountability, and modeled behavior. When leaders relax standards in the name of trust without first establishing a foundation of discipline, the results are predictable and often costly. Alcohol doesn't create problems on its own; lax leadership amplifies them. The fix starts with owning the environment you allow.

Some of us senior NCOs warned against allowing Soldiers to store alcohol in their rooms, but the command team dismissed the advice. Ignoring the fact that many of our junior leaders and some senior leaders were on their *first* deployment and still learning how to lead themselves, let alone others. What they experienced instead was a complete breakdown of discipline and standards.

Consider the long-term impact: those junior leaders will carry that first example with them as they advance in the Army. That chaotic, undisciplined environment becomes their baseline for what "normal" looks like. Not the best start. We can't take back our poor decisions; we can learn from them and correct our ways.

By the time the command team finally tried to crack down, it was far too late, nothing more than a band-aid slapped over a femoral artery bleed. Once discipline erodes, it does not stop on its own. It accelerates. What begins as a relaxed standard becomes a tolerated standard and eventually becomes the new norm. By the time the problems surface in full, it is too late—the culture has already collapsed.

Watching that unfold taught me more about leadership than any manual ever could. It showed me exactly what happens when standards are not enforced, when NCOs are ignored, and when leaders choose convenience over discipline. More importantly, it taught me how **not** to run an organization.

The answer is simple in theory but demanding in execution: **you set the standard early, enforce it consistently, and communicate relentlessly.** Culture doesn't emerge by accident; it is designed, spoken into existence, reinforced, and modeled.

Let us take this as a case study and turn back the clock. What would you do to start this deployment? How would you establish the culture of a newly formed organization as it embarks on a deployment?

Rewinding the Clock: How to Build Culture the Right Way

Looking back on that deployment, it's easy to play the Monday morning quarterback. Hindsight is generous like that. But if I had been sitting on the command team, operating within my proper sphere of influence, there are things I would have done differently, deliberately and immediately. Not because doctrine said so, but because culture doesn't wait for leaders to get comfortable. It forms regardless of your readiness.

Before wheels leave the ground, we are crystal clear about the organization we intend to run—we establish a core command philosophy, we needed clear purpose. Not in slogans. Not in vague phrases that sound good during briefings, but in clear expectations. What does discipline actually look like in this context? When no one is watching, what does accountability mean? What behaviors are non-negotiable? How are rumors handled? How is friction addressed? What values must every Soldier demonstrate daily, not just when leadership is present? If leaders do not define those answers themselves, the formation does it for them—and it always chooses whatever is easiest, not whatever is right. Once we set the core of the organization, we ensure those expectations are communicated consistently and reinforced relentlessly.

That clarity only matters if the command team presents a single, unified front. Culture collapses the moment Soldiers hear mixed messages. "The commander said one thing, but the First Sergeant said another." "The XO lets it slide, but the platoon sergeant doesn't." Those cracks don't stay small. Soldiers find them, exploit them, and widen them until standards no longer mean anything. Disagreements within the command team are inevitable, but they must be settled behind closed doors. Once leaders step in front of the formation, they are one organism, with one voice and one spine. Anything less invites unmanaged chaos.

You must establish discipline early, before it becomes necessary. If it isn't built on day-one, the rest of the year will be spent chasing it. Accountability formations, uniform inspections, standards briefings, and clear consequences aren't signs of distrust; they're signs of leadership. You can't wait for a problem and then suddenly decide to get strict. Soldiers can smell inconsistency from a mile away. Culture is built through repeated enforcement, not motivational speeches. And yes, sometimes enforcing standards carries personal or career risks. But that risk should be accepted consciously, not forced on leaders because discipline was neglected early.

The environment matters and must be factored in. Privileges, especially alcohol, must be controlled or not introduced at all. Formal, structured events like dining-ins can serve a purpose, but during regular operations, especially in a newly formed or deploying unit, structure must take precedence over comfort. You never introduce a privilege you are unwilling or unable to control. Leaders set the rules, validate the rules, and enforce the rules. If they don't, what they get isn't morale; it's disorder masquerading as freedom.

None of this works without a strong NCO corps. NCOs are the shock absorbers of the organization and its greatest force multipliers. Ignoring their advice is the fastest way to cripple a unit. From day one, NCOs must be empowered with proper authority, real responsibility, and visible backing from the command team. A deployment lives or dies on the strength of its NCOs. Trust them, but if an NCO violates that trust, act decisively and remove them. Culture cannot survive selective enforcement.

Rituals and identity matter more than people think. Daily formations early on build rhythm and accountability, even if they're reduced later. Clean, disciplined barracks reinforce pride and order. Professional communication standards set expectations for how Soldiers treat one another. Company mottos, symbols, and shared identity, when rooted in Army values, give people something to belong to. Wins should be celebrated publicly. Corrections should happen privately. These rituals reinforce a sense of belonging, and a sense of belonging reinforces discipline.

Outstanding leaders don't stop at explaining what needs to be done or how to do it. They explain why. Especially in deployment environments, where stress, fatigue, and homesickness amplify every emotion, understanding the purpose behind standards makes all the difference. Soldiers are far more likely to uphold expectations and hold each other accountable when they understand the reason behind them. When expectations aren't met, frustration isn't the answer. Clarity is. Make the unspoken spoken. Clarity beats anger every time.

Ultimately, culture isn't built through guidance or emails. It's built through presence. Leaders have to be visible. Walk the barracks. Sit in on squad huddles. Visit guard towers at one in the morning. Eat in the chow hall with Soldiers. Your presence reinforces standards. Your absence gives permission. When you see something out of place or unauthorized, correct it immediately. Don't walk past it. Don't promise to address it later. This isn't new advice; you have heard it before. The difference is whether you **act** on it.

If I could turn the clock back on that deployment, I would anchor everything to one simple principle: culture is not what you say, it's what you enforce. And what you enforce begins on Day One. Even though I wasn't in a formal command position during that deployment, I had years of experience and lessons learned that were not being put into practice. The organizational culture collapsed because standards were never established, never protected, and never enforced. Culture drifted, discipline crumbled, and the organization paid the price. Fortunately, that unit was a temporary task force, not a long-standing, historically rich one, but even the most storied organizations can struggle under poor leadership.

If we had acted decisively on every lapse in discipline from day one, the deployment would have gone differently. Culture is not built by words—it is enforced through actions. Alcohol? Fine—but only at sanctioned events. No drinking in living areas or during work hours. Every expectation, every standard, every correction compounds. Get it right from the start, and the unit not only survives the chaos, it thrives, accomplishing the mission while building trust, cohesion, and pride.

Building a strong culture is not complicated—but it *requires* leaders who genuinely care and who will take consistent action. Culture doesn't magically appear because a commander gives a speech or because the unit prints a motto on a t-shirt. Culture is shaped by what leaders do, what they overlook, and what they allow to slip—day after day.

Human factors matter here. In a deployed environment, stress is higher, sleep is lower, patience is thinner, and personal problems are magnified. That means minor lapses in discipline don't just stay small; they **grow fast** because the environment accelerates everything. A minor issue in garrison becomes a major issue downrange. A vague standard at home gives rise to chaos overseas.

And yes—cultures that are shaped by unclear intent, inconsistent enforcement, or leaders who avoid hard conversations will absolutely drift off course. Human beings fill voids with their own interpretations. When leadership fails to define a culture, the group will build one on its own—and it usually won't be the one you wanted.

But here's the good news: azimuths can be reset. Leaders can course-correct a drifting culture if they act quickly, consistently, and with clarity. That means confronting minor problems before they become normalized behaviors. It means tightening standards **before** Soldiers decide what the standard is for themselves.

And most importantly, it means recognizing that an unhealthy culture doesn't heal on its own—**it festers.**

You build the culture you enforce.

You enforce the culture you care about.

And you protect the culture by acting the moment it drifts.

If leaders commit to those actions, not once, not occasionally, but constantly, the culture will grow stronger, healthier, and more resilient. And if they don't? The culture will build itself, and chances are, you won't like the result.

Wrapping It Up

Trust is not an abstract leadership concept; it is built, reinforced, or destroyed through deliberate actions taken every single day. In this chapter, we walked through the reality that trust doesn't begin in grand gestures or crisis moments; it starts in the ordinary, routine, and often overlooked spaces where leaders show or don't.

The first formation, the opening meeting, the initial interaction of the day, are leadership touchpoints that quietly shape culture. When leaders treat them as sacred, purposeful moments, they set clarity, energy, and direction. When they treat them as administrative chores or delegate them away, they give up one of the easiest opportunities to build trust. Presence matters. Consistency matters, and the tone you set early carries farther than most leaders realize.

Stepping into senior leadership also means accepting a truth many people underestimate: you are a public figure now. Whether or not you want the spotlight, it exists. Your words, actions, discipline, and professionalism are always being observed, interpreted, and repeated. Professionalism becomes your armor—it protects your credibility when scrutiny increases and when mistakes happen.

Leaders who understand this use their visibility to lift their organization. Leaders who ignore it are often surprised when the narrative turns against them.

Culture, whether military or civilian, does not form by accident. It becomes what leaders project, reinforce, and protect. If you do not actively shape the narrative of your organization, someone else will—and they may not do it in a way that aligns with your values or intent. Trust grows when leaders speak with clarity, act with consistency, and align their words with their actions. It erodes when standards are vague, enforcement is selective, or leadership avoids hard conversations.

Perhaps the hardest lesson in this chapter is this: trust without discipline is not trust; it is neglect. Relaxed standards, inconsistent enforcement, and misplaced "flexibility" do not empower people; they confuse them. Excellent organizations establish discipline early, enforce it fairly, and explain the why behind it. Discipline does not stifle trust; it enables it. It creates predictability, safety, and a shared understanding.

Culture collapse never happens all at once. It happens through small decisions, ignored warnings, and leaders choosing convenience over consistency. But the reverse is also true: a strong culture is built through early action, unified leadership, visible presence, and immediate correction when things drift. Leaders don't get to wait until problems feel big enough to address. By then, it's already too late.

Trust is the currency that carries you through chaos, conflict, and uncertainty. It allows organizations to move faster, recover quicker, and endure stress without fracturing. But trust is fragile. It must be earned continuously and protected aggressively.

In the end, trust is not what you say, it is what you enforce. It is not what you intend, it is what your people experience.

It is not built in comfort; it is built in consistency.

Lead deliberately. Show up early. Set the tone. Protect the culture.

This is the foundation for building trust, establishing organizational culture, and the reason it endures.

Chapter Four

Leading in Chaos

How to find and fix the friction points that are attempting to ruin your plans

> "The 1SG can solve 99% of friction with these three things: an LMTV, trash bags, and folding tables."

Anyone who has served with me knows I swear by that quote. It sounds like a joke, and I deliver it like one, but it's rooted in decades of observing what actually derails training, missions, and morale. Those three items represent something deeper: anticipation, preparation, and the ability to create order from chaos.

I operate the **Light Medium Tactical Vehicle (LMTV),** the Army's reliable workhorse and true unsung hero. This platform efficiently transports troops, hauls essential equipment, and delivers personnel and supplies directly to points of need, even under demanding conditions. Admittedly, the LMTV isn't designed for comfort or curb appeal. Its ride can be punishing thanks to a no-nonsense suspension, the cab is utilitarian at best, and its silhouette is unmistakably functional rather than sleek. Yet when the alternative is a long foot march, especially under load, in heat, or over rough terrain, soldiers rarely hesitate to climb aboard.

Trash bags, never underestimate them, because units generate more trash than you think, and you can never have enough on hand.

Folding tables provide a proper surface to serve chow in the field, boosting morale and professionalism. We're not a low-brow grunt outfit; at least we have enough class not to eat off the ground.

But these items are just tools of the trade. The actual work of a 1SG is **sensing the friction to transform chaos into opportunity**. You are the organization's pressure gauge. You are expected to see friction before it surfaces, feel problems before they erupt, and read both the physical and human terrain to understand where things are about to go sideways.

This isn't mysticism. Employing wizardry or reading tea leaves is not involved here. This is **pattern recognition**. It's experience within your organization. It's watching Soldiers, the plan, the environment, and the timeline all at once, and noticing what doesn't line up.

For inexperienced senior leaders, friction can feel elusive. Problems seem to appear out of nowhere. But with time and deliberate observation, you see early indicators: confused faces, missing resources, unclear timelines, or plans that depend too heavily on everything going perfectly. The best way to find friction is to know the plan.

Command Team Reality: You have to help your commander with the plan. You cannot let them operate in a silo and hope everyone magically has the right information. That's not leadership; it's blind optimism dressed up as delegation. A strong 1SG doesn't just execute the plan; they **shape it**. They ask probing questions early, identify gaps before they become problems, and ensure the plan reflects how people actually function, not how it looks on paper.

In the field, a few critical realities stand out:

Are your Soldiers truly prepared for the tasks ahead, or only theoretically ready?

Have you identified and eliminated friction points before they touch the formation, or, at the very least, built contingencies to neutralize them the moment they appear?

Friction is inevitable. It's not a question of if, but when. An accurate measure of leadership is whether your team is ready to absorb it.

It's easy to write this down on paper, but it's far harder to manage in reality. Pre-combat checks and inspections may confirm that Soldiers have all their gear, but reality has a way of exposing those pesky hidden gaps. You may find yourself in the field needing to change a vehicle tire and realize there's no jack. Or a communication plan looks perfect in a briefing, only to find that we somehow forgot the batteries. These are the moments that separate theoretical readiness from actual operational effectiveness.

There are ten million friction points out there that all have a singular purpose: to ruin your day! The aim is to help shape that friction-point intuition so that you, as the senior leader, can anticipate issues before they become crises and prevent gaps in operations. This is the essence of proactive leadership, transforming experience and foresight into actionable solutions that keep the mission moving and Soldiers safe. Understanding these dynamics at the company level directly informs our approach to Army operations.

Current Operations (CUOPS) and Future Operations (FUOPS)–Managing Today While Shaping Tomorrow

In Army operations, everything revolves around two critical functions: **Current Operations (CUOPS)** and **Future Operations (FUOPS)**[5]. I've always viewed the command team relationship through that lens:

CUOPS is the chaos in front of you.

FUOPS is the strategy that shapes what comes next.

As the 1SG or the senior leader of your outfit, you focus your fight on CUOPS so your commander has the bandwidth to build FUOPS. That balance isn't just efficient; it's the backbone of a functional, disciplined, and agile organization. Even though the 1SG's focus is on CUOPS, you are not entirely out of FUOPS. The 1SG is often the most experienced NCO in the company, and that experience shapes tomorrow's reality. Help the commander understand what's realistic, workable, and achievable over the course of the training year.

For example, a 12-mile foot march in January in Yakima, Washington sounds motivating on paper, but reality matters. Weather, terrain, and unit readiness must guide the plan. FUOPS needs **realism**. CUOPS needs **control**. And the 1SG sits at the intersection of both, fighting today while helping the Commander shape tomorrow.

Developing Your Friction Point Intuition

You do not arrive in the 1SG seat with an instinct for every friction point already formed. That awareness is built slowly through repetition, observation, and a careful study of how your unit functions under stress. Each organization develops its own "fingerprint of friction," influenced by fatigue, pressure, and human behavior. More often than not, the first indicator is something simple; missing resources.

Most of my experience comes from Infantry companies, where friction commonly shows up in movement, ammunition, timelines, chow, and communications. Other formations, aviation, engineers, sustainers, face entirely different pressure points. What feels routine in one unit may be a full-blown crisis in another. Take the time to develop an understanding of your specific organization and accept that no two formations operate the same way.

Do not assume prior experience transfers perfectly. Study your formation. Ask questions. Observe. Pay attention to signs of stress, confusion, and missed details. This is how you build intuition for friction points, not overnight, not by assumption, but through deliberate attention and experience. Missing resources, though, is the best indicator for you to ask some probing questions.

While deliberate observation and experience remain the surest path to developing sharp friction point intuition, certain high-intensity training scenarios can compress years of lessons into days—or even hours. They force leaders to confront chaos head-on, exposing hidden stressors, resource gaps, and decision points in real time.

One such scenario has lingered in my mind for years: an idealized training event I've envisioned but never fully seen executed. It deliberately engineers the very conditions that accelerate intuition-building, turning theoretical awareness into hard-won instinct. I am hoping one day a unit will bring it to life. Maybe your outfit already has. I just know I never got to execute this one. The intent of this training event is to set the conditions for leaders at every level to experience a training environment that tests their ability to lead in chaos. Looking at this mission from the senior leader's perspective, it builds your friction intuition quickly.

This training event would be resource-heavy and demanding to plan, but that is precisely why it would be ideal for a senior Platoon Sergeant to own from start to finish. By resourcing, coordinating, and executing it, the PSG would gain unmatched visibility into the team's current readiness, exposing gaps and holes that might otherwise remain hidden.

Now, let's bring that vision to life. We'll step into the world of imagination and walk through an example of what this training event is and how this event could be put into practice. If you have ever experienced Mountain Phase of Ranger school, this mission would seem a bit familiar.

My Perfect Training Event Example

To set the scene, this is a drill weekend that begins like countless others. It is a standard three-day training event, starting early Friday morning with Soldiers reporting to the armory in Washington State. The plan is routine and familiar: movement to the Yakima Training Center and three days of patrol operations in a large, well-known training area.

Nothing on the schedule feels unusual. Vehicles are staged. Packing lists are checked. Leaders brief timelines everyone has heard before. Most of the Soldiers have trained on this ground many times, and the mission set—patrols, movement, security—fits neatly within expectations. On paper, it is a clean weekend with few surprises.

That sense of normalcy matters because it is exactly what makes what happens next matter.

Right before loading vehicles, the platoon leaders are called over separately.

No speeches. No theatrics. Just a fragmentary order slid across the table that quietly changes the entire weekend. The mission changes—a Fragmentary Order, or FRAGO. Here is the new scenario: a helicopter has gone down inside the training area. Two pilots are missing. Their condition is unknown. The area is hostile, with enemy forces already moving toward the crash site. Speed matters. Stealth matters more.

The normal drop-off point is no longer viable. Instead, the platoons insert farther north, into less familiar ground. The terrain punishes lazy planning and rewards leaders who pay attention to detail. Along with enough information to understand they are no longer running standard training lanes, the team receives the aircraft's last known location.

The platoon leaders and platoon sergeants break away and go to work. Information moves fast and imperfectly, just as it does in the real world. Soldiers are told what matters and nothing more to preserve time for preparation. The mission has changed. Time is compressed. Enemy contact is imminent. The platoons plan accordingly.

We see which platoon uses the time in transit to inform their Soldiers and refine their plans.

By the time the platoons step off the trucks, the shift in mindset is visible. Movement is no longer casual. Leaders read the terrain instead of checking boxes. They choose routes for concealment, not convenience. They factor in darkness to mask movement.

The platoons reach their first checkpoint, and enemy contact follows. Enemy scouts probe their movement, forcing quick reactions. Formations adjust to enemy tactics. Leaders build control measures on the fly. As pressure increases, they use attached mortars as a problem-solving tool, not a scripted event. Fires create space, but they also announce presence. From that point forward, the clock speeds up.

As the platoons push closer to the crash site, the tempo shifts again. Security becomes deliberate. Leaders slow things down just enough to understand what they are walking into. The crash site must be taken by force. They secure the area, push back enemy elements, and begin the real work.

They find both pilots alive but unable to walk. Medics treat them immediately and prepare them for movement. Security elements establish positions along likely avenues of approach. Decisions are made with incomplete information and tired minds. The team discusses evacuation routes and reworks timelines. Nothing about the plan survives first contact, but the mission remains the same. Air support is turned off for the night—no medical evacuation is coming. They establish a patrol base to reset.

When movement resumes early the next morning, it is heavier. Slower. Harder. The enemy harasses them through the night and presses the withdrawal, forcing the platoons to fight their way out while protecting casualties. Miles of movement follow through terrain that punishes mistakes and magnifies small leadership failures.

Eventually, they secure a landing zone. A single helicopter arrives. The team loads the two injured pilots. For a moment, it feels like the mission is over.

Then the weather turns.

Air assets shut down. No more lifts. No clean exit. The platoons fight their way out. Packs go back on. Routes are re-evaluated. The mission shifts from extraction to endurance. Leaders stay forward. They make corrections quietly. Movement continues.

On the last day of drill, the platoons emerge at the final pickup site—not to spinning rotors, but to two buses waiting to take them home.

No dramatic ending. No applause. Just tired, dirty Soldiers with worn boots, and leaders who think, adapt, and carry responsibility when it matters.

This is the drill I want to run—not because it is complex or resource-heavy, but because it is honest. It gives platoons room to lead, space to fail, and enough friction to expose strengths and weaknesses no checklist ever will. More importantly, it gives them a sense of accomplishment, earned through effort, decision-making, and shared hardship, that stays with them long after the weekend ends.

That's where real training lives: between the plan you wrote and the reality you did not predict.

Assessing the Friction Points of My Training Event

Now, let us assess the friction points that these platoons will encounter, the friction the 1SG needs to expect. Remember, the platoons can only go as far as you can sustain them.

In every operation, the fight does not begin at the objective; it begins long before wheels ever roll. It is not the first sergeant's job to command platoons or micromanage them. The role is quieter: ensuring the operation never stalls because of something predictable or preventable. The focus is not on tactics first, but on systems to keep the men fighting long past first contact with the enemy.

Movement is the first place friction appears. Vehicles break down, convoys bunch up, drivers miss turns, and one disabled truck can halt an entire operation if contingency plans are absent. A competent first sergeant ensures recovery assets are staged, not requested. Spare tires, jacks, and tools must be present and accounted for. Plans must define who stays, who moves, and how accountability is maintained when a vehicle inevitably fails. If a platoon halts because a jack is missing, the failure lies not with the soldiers but with the systems that were not reinforced.

Sustainment becomes the next silent adversary. Platoons rarely fail because they cannot maneuver, they fail because they run out of energy. Water disappears faster than planned. MREs are consumed too quickly or hoarded. Fatigue sets in, and equipment breaks down. The First Sergeant tracks consumption and behavior proactively. Resupply is pushed forward at the right time and place, keeping the platoons moving while allowing leaders to retain ownership of the mission.

Medical issues present another friction point that rarely announce themselves dramatically. Minor injuries, a rolled ankle, heat exhaustion, and a blister can derail training if overlooked. Evacuation routes, casualty collection points, and medical redundancy must be established in advance. A platoon should never face a choice between mission success and the health of its soldiers, because the First Sergeant anticipated those challenges.

Communications are equally fragile. Radios fail, terrain blocks signals, and batteries die. Silence is dangerous. When communication falters, corrective actions must be immediate: repositioning, sending runners, or moving sustainment elements forward to reestablish contact. The goal is not to fix the radios but to recognize when communication gaps threaten operational momentum.

Time itself is a friction point. Everything takes longer than planned. Movement slows, casualty treatment delays, and reorganization under stress burn hours. A skilled First Sergeant assesses whether platoons fall behind because of friction or indecision. Intervention can mean applying pressure or buying time through sustainment, security, or quiet guidance. Recognizing the difference is essential.

The most insidious friction, however, is leader fatigue. Platoon sergeants and squad leaders must be closely monitored for signs of exhaustion, lapses in delegation, or rising frustration. Interventions, such as redistributing responsibility, enforcing short breaks, or adjusting tasks, preserve combat power without undermining authority.

A fundamental principle governs effective First Sergeant leadership: if a platoon stalls because of logistics, sustainment, or preventable friction, the responsibility lies with those who support the fight, not those executing it. Success is measured by what never happens: no mission paused for water, no training halted for missing equipment, no platoon crushed under cumulative minor problems.

In this framework, platoons own the fight. The First Sergeant owns everything that allows them to continue. Developing this friction-point intuition means seeing problems before they touch the formation and neutralizing them while preserving the autonomy and agency of the leaders executing the mission. This mission won't expose all the gaps in your outfit, but it will be an excellent start to finding the biggest ones.

Sustainment From the Administrative Perspective

I usually operate with two minds: one administrative and one tactical. On the administrative side, my focus is logistics and sustainment—planning how we get to the training site, securing the necessary resources to support the event, arranging transportation, chow, and portable chemical latrines (PCLs). I track headcounts: how many Soldiers are in each platoon? Do we have enough seats on the trucks to move all the personnel plus the equipment required for the training exercise? Every detail matters to ensure the unit arrives ready, stays fed and hygienic, and doesn't lose momentum because of preventable shortfalls. Remember, these are the senior leader concerns.

When teams are developing their plans, these are the probing questions I ask early, before friction has a chance to take root. None of them are complicated, but every one of them matters.

How are the Soldiers getting paid?

This is a budgetary question that cannot be an afterthought. Are orders correct? Is funding approved? Are entitlements clear? If pay becomes a problem, morale will follow close behind.

How are we getting there?

This is a transportation problem, not a scheduling one. Are we using commercial buses or tactical vehicles? Do we have licensed drivers? Recovery assets? A movement plan that assumes nothing will break is not a plan.

What are we eating?

Class I is always a friction point. Chow plans require redundancy. Are meals provided? Are travel funds authorized? Are MREs staged as a backup? Hungry Soldiers stop listening long before they stop moving.

Where are Soldiers sleeping?

Barracks or field? Tents or trucks? Have we confirmed Soldiers actually have the right equipment for the environment they're entering? Exposure, fatigue, and poor rest will degrade performance faster than most tactical problems.

And finally—where is the poop going?

This is not a joke question. Latrine planning can become a logistical and health nightmare if it's ignored. If you don't account for it early, it will force its way into the plan later, and it will not be pretty.

Why this works?

These questions don't constrain creativity, they protect it. When these fundamentals are addressed, platoon leadership can focus on tactics instead of fighting preventable sustainment problems. This is how a First Sergeant turns a concept into a plan that survives contact with reality.

Sustainment From a Tactical Perspective

From a tactical perspective, it's all about the fight and the training value. Have we coordinated opposing forces (OPFOR), and are they properly sustained and positioned? Do we have a clear tactical order that outlines the enemy situation, scheme of maneuver, and key intelligence? What training aids are at my disposal to enhance the outcome—smoke, pyrotechnics, integration of Multiple Integrated Laser Engagement System (MILES) gear? Do we have sufficient blank rounds, simunitions, or other munitions? Are there any attachments or enablers attached—forward observers, scouts, engineers, or additional fire support—to make the training more realistic and effective? These issues are 100% the First Sergeant's to own and solve. You don't get to pass them off—this one's on you.

When thinking about logistics at the tactical level, I use the **Shoot, Move, and Communicate** thought model to frame the probing questions I ask of myself and platoon leadership. It is a simple structure, but it helps in planning and quickly exposes gaps that will create friction later. These are some of the probing questions I ask using this thought model:

Shoot

Do we have assigned weapons for every Soldier and are they serviceable? Do we have enough magazines, Cleaner-Lubricant-Preservative (CLP), and range boxes to sustain operations beyond the first engagement? If vehicles are involved, do we have the correct mounting hardware for crew-served weapons? Can we fight at night? Lasers, night vision devices, batteries, and weapon sight zeros all matter. This list can grow quickly, but its purpose is not to be exhaustive, it is to prompt the right questions before those omissions surface under stress.

Quick Note: My company is commonly fighting understrength, meaning we do not have enough Soldiers to fill every position, but we are still expected to fight as a full company. How do we do this? We ensure every machine gun is checked out of the arms room. If that means a Squad Leader has to sling a Squad Automatic Weapon (SAW) and fight as a gunner, then that's exactly what happens. We win the firefight by outgunning whoever we face.

Move

Do we have the required vehicles, and have they been properly checked and maintained? Are Soldiers licensed and trained on the platforms they will operate? Can the unit move at night? If vehicles are unavailable, can the formation move on foot for extended distances? Are Soldiers physically conditioned for that movement? Mobility is not just about transportation—it is about endurance, adaptability, and redundancy.

Communicate

Can we communicate over long distances and complex terrain? What is our primary, alternate, contingent, and emergent (PACE) plan, and does everyone understand it? Can we power our communication systems for the duration of the mission? Do we have the correct frequencies and crypto fills loaded and verified? If all communications fail, have we established time-based or action-based triggers to keep the mission moving?

This thought model gives me a disciplined way to assess logistics through a tactical lens. It does not replace planning, it sharpens it. By deliberately walking through Shoot, Move, and Communicate, I can identify friction early and ensure platoon leaders are set up to fight the mission, not the systems that support it.

Why This Works?

This model works because it mirrors how Soldiers actually experience combat and training, sequentially, under stress, and with imperfect information. Shoot, Move, and Communicate is not an abstract framework; it is the reality of every tactical problem a platoon faces once contact is made. When logistics are framed this way, gaps become obvious because they are tied directly to action, not checklists. A missing battery is no longer a supply oversight, it is a platoon that cannot fight at night. An unlicensed driver is not a training deficiency, it is a formation that cannot reposition when it matters most.

For a senior leader, this model enforces discipline without slowing momentum. It keeps planning grounded in execution and prevents logistics from becoming an afterthought. More importantly, it aligns sustainment with trust. When platoon leadership sees that the systems supporting them are reliable, they are free to focus on leadership and decision-making. That confidence allows units to move faster, adapt sooner, and absorb friction without breaking. Shoot, Move, and Communicate doesn't eliminate friction, but it ensures that when friction appears, it isn't because something predictable was ignored.

Wrapping It Up

At the end of the day, leadership at the company level comes down to one principle: success is measured not by what went right, but by what never went wrong. A First Sergeant's role is rarely glamorous, often invisible, yet indispensable. The LMTV, the trash bags, and the folding tables are more than tools, they are symbols of anticipation, preparation, and the ability to create order from chaos. They are small pieces of a larger truth: a well-led formation never waits for problems to manifest; it prevents them.

Friction is inevitable. Vehicles will break down. Radios will fail. Soldiers will become exhausted. Supplies will dwindle. Injuries will occur. Time will compress. And when these pressures collide, the First Sergeant is the constant, ensuring that the mission moves forward, the Soldiers are sustained, and leadership remains effective. The 1SG does not remove friction; they channel it, absorb it, and, when necessary, neutralize it before it derails the operation.

This is where intuition is earned. Friction-point awareness is not a skill that can be acquired overnight. It comes through repetition, observation, and deliberate engagement with the formation. It grows from studying the plan, monitoring behavior, anticipating needs, and asking the hard questions before anyone else does. The First Sergeant shapes the battlefield not by standing at the front, but by ensuring that everything behind the frontline functions seamlessly. In doing so, the platoons retain the autonomy to execute, adapt, and succeed.

Current Operations and Future Operations are inseparable in this framework. CUOPS, the chaos of today, demands immediate attention. FUOPS, the strategy of tomorrow, depends on the space and clarity that CUOPS management provides. A skilled 1SG operates at the intersection, balancing the present while shaping the future, ensuring plans are feasible, realistic, and aligned with both the environment and the people executing them.

Ultimately, leadership is about presence, foresight, and relentless accountability. Platoons own the fight; the First Sergeant owns everything that allows them to continue. Culture, discipline, morale, and operational success are all reflections of how friction is managed. The greatest leaders are not those who react flawlessly to chaos; they are those who see it coming, prepare for it, and shape it into a force multiplier.

In this light, every tool, every inspection, every minor correction becomes part of a larger mission: sustaining the unit, empowering leaders, and ensuring the mission succeeds. The First Sergeant's currency is trust, experience, and the quiet, relentless management of friction. Master that, and the unit will not only survive, but it will also thrive, even when the unexpected becomes inevitable.

Chapter Five

Building Lethal and High-Performing Teams

Empowering Others to Step Up

> "Plan to work yourself out of a job."

Developing Individual Leaders

If I say **Noncommissioned Officer Professional Development (NCOPD)**, what's the first thing that comes to mind?

I'll take a guess. It's a classroom somewhere, with a PowerPoint flickering on the screen, and the discussion is about topics that seem to have zero effect on readiness. Everyone's nodding politely, some are pretending to take notes, a few are completely asleep, and all of them are counting the minutes until it's over. It's just a guess, maybe your experiences with NCO professional development have been way better, and you've had truly impactful development over your tenure. If that's the case, great. But we're still going to cover some lessons I learned as a senior leader.

I can almost guarantee that nobody woke up in the morning excited for **NCOPD.** If it were possible to measure enthusiasm, most of you would rank this between flu shots and personal record review for the third time this year. And that's fair. NCO Professional Development has earned its reputation over the years.

Too often, NCO Professional Development feels like death by PowerPoint. Recycled slides, vague leadership quotes attributed to people who were never NCOs, and a discussion period that comprises one motivated Staff Sergeant talking to himself while everyone else is taking an inventory of the back of their eyelids.

NCO professional development isn't the problem. How we've been doing it is.

When people treat NCO professional development as a check-the-box requirement, it becomes exactly that, another mandatory event that drains time and delivers nothing. When it's treated as leader development, it becomes one of the most powerful tools we have. The difference isn't resources, rank, or doctrine. It's intent.

Development requires effort. But if we do this right, you'll leave with something useful: tools your leaders can apply Monday morning, not concepts they forget by lunch.

Let's do this the way NCOs are supposed to: practical, direct, and grounded in what works.

I've been fortunate to serve as a 1SG for over six years in the same battalion, and it was during my third time as a company 1SG that I had a real epiphany about developing leaders in a part-time force. Yes, it was my third go, I am not the quickest learner. One of the biggest lessons I learned is that it's okay not to get it right the first time—as long as you are deliberately striving to improve and hone your leadership skills, you are on the right track.

My approach began with the development of the company's annual training plan, helping my commander build a realistic and achievable training path. We would spend hours reviewing higher command's intent, identifying key tasks, and finding training opportunities to fill gaps. But instead of the command team shouldering the full burden, I designed a concept that allowed junior NCOs to take ownership of portions of the plan. This wasn't assigning them low-stakes, zero-consequence NCO Professional Development (NCOPD) classes; this was real training with tangible outcomes. If they failed, it mattered—and that reality helped build accountability and buy-in.

This is how I structured it:

· **E-5s** handled flat ranges or qualification ranges, which was a routine event for our organization. While not complicated in theory, it still needed careful planning and resource management. I created conditions that allowed them time to plan, gather resources, execute, and learn from minor failures without catastrophic consequences. If they forgot to factor in how the ammunition point was going to run, I would stand back and watch how they handled applying quick-fix reaction decisions on site.

· **E-6s** managed more complex exercises, such as Squad Situational Training Exercise (STX) lanes. No live fire, just blank rounds, but still required both tactical and logistical planning. Squad leaders scheduled the training, coordinated resources, and executed the training. This gave them practical experience running more complex operations and provided opportunities to make decisions under pressure.

· **E-7s** took on live-fire events and platoon maneuvers. This level required them to plan at the platoon level, integrating multiple squads and assets. My intent is simple: **how can a platoon sergeant effectively advise a platoon leader if they've never actually planned a complex training exercise?** NCOs must have hands-on planning experience to gain the insight necessary to mentor junior officers.

You may have noticed that this structured development lands squarely in the sustainment from the administrative perspective we discussed in the last chapter. That is exactly right, if you master planning an administrative training event, the tactical version becomes second nature, the framework's the same, just swap the outcomes.

This tiered structure created a real-world progression of responsibility, allowing each level of NCO to build competence, confidence, and credibility. By giving NCOs meaningful, consequence-driven leadership tasks, they developed the knowledge and experience to advise leaders above and below them, and most importantly, to contribute directly to the company's success.

Another benefit of assigning these types of training events is that you quickly see who cares and who doesn't. Those who engage, plan, and take ownership stand out. The ones who don't care reveal themselves just as fast. When that happens, take action—remove them from positions of influence and provide a clear pathway for them to make better choices or exit the unit if necessary. It protects the rest of the Soldiers and preserves the integrity of the team.

It is okay to "fire" or remove team leaders and squad leaders from their positions if it serves their development. When that happens, they typically face two paths: the first is to sulk and adopt a "woe is me" attitude and quit. The second, and the ideal outcome, is that it sparks motivation, lights a fire under them, and drives them to improve. This approach ensures meaningful leadership development, and that growth directly links to accountability. You may need to guide that pathway to motivation as the senior leader. Quitting is the simplest option; don't make it the easiest.

This approach works because leadership is best learned by doing, not just by observing or listening in a classroom. Giving NCOs real responsibility with tangible consequences forces them to think critically, make decisions under pressure, and understand the cascading effects of their actions. It transforms abstract concepts from doctrine and PowerPoints into practical experience. By structuring development in progressive tiers—where E-5s, E-6s, and E-7s each own increasingly complex portions of the plan, leaders learn not only how to execute but also how to anticipate, advise, and shape outcomes. When NCOs face challenges crucial to the mission, unit, and the Soldiers they lead, they experience genuine professional development. They also must feel the consequences if they fail.

Remember this: when you are stateside and in a training environment and a mission fails, that is exactly where you want it to fail. That is the purpose of training. Failure in garrison or stateside is not a catastrophe; think of it as a big classroom. We didn't make it to the moon on the first rocket, and no unit becomes lethal, disciplined, or adaptive by getting everything right the first time. Honest reflection and correction follow failures, which leaders who care observe. You just have to set the conditions to allow failure to happen.

This method gets my NCOs thinking critically about how to get to the fight and—more importantly—how to sustain it once they're there. But that's only part of the equation. I take a different, more focused approach to tactical development.

I got asked once: "How do you rack and stack your NCOs in your company?" Dead simple: In my company, a leader's worth is measured by whether their platoon, squad, or team can pull off a perfect ambush, raid, or patrol base—one offensive surprise attack, one offensive objective seizure, and one defensive security setup. These aren't the whole infantry playbook; they're focused, realistic training priorities that force mastery of mission-essential tasks without dilution. Fitness, schools, administrative mastery? Secondary. If they can't train their teams to own the fight when it counts, they're not stacking high on my list. Period.

That standard pushes NCOs to self-train hard: digging into doctrine, drilling independently, and holding their teams accountable. It ultimately reveals who can truly lead, those who validate their skills by training squads and platoons to execute complex tactical missions flawlessly. When their team performs because they trained them to, that's the proof. That's what earns honest top-block ratings and builds a lethal unit.

The Implied Task Drought

A recurring statement I've heard from several high-level senior leaders in our organization is that "there are no implied tasks in a National Guard unit." I respectfully, but firmly disagree. This perspective, while perhaps intended to promote clarity and reduce risk in a part-time force, ultimately undermines the very development we need most: agile, creative, critical-thinking leaders who can operate effectively in ambiguous, high-stakes environments.

By declaring that no implied tasks exist, we send an implicit message to our Soldiers and junior leaders: you cannot—or should not—be trusted to think independently. You must be given explicit, step-by-step directions with zero room for interpretation or initiative. This approach contradicts core Army doctrine. ADP 6-0 Mission Command philosophy explicitly defines mission command as the exercise of authority through mission orders that enable disciplined initiative within the commander's intent[6]. Implied tasks, those derived from mission analysis, terrain, enemy, and civil considerations, are not optional; they are fundamental to decentralized execution and adaptive leadership.

In a National Guard context, where training windows are short and real-world operations often unfold unpredictably, denying implied tasks becomes a shortcut, a cop-out that avoids the harder work of building shared understanding, fostering mutual trust, and accepting prudent risk. It stifles growth by prioritizing control over empowerment. Junior leaders who are never expected to infer, prioritize, or adapt will never develop the judgment needed when plans inevitably change.

I hope we can change this perspective to a more soldier-centric message. Instead of asking how to eliminate ambiguity, our senior leaders should ask a better question:

"How can we set the conditions for decision-making at the lowest possible level?"

I have already provided a solution to how we can do this in the last chapter, which I explained in "my perfect training event." It provides the right amount of space for leaders to make decisions, feel the consequences of their decisions, and learn from their mistakes. This is all designed to develop lethal teams in a controlled training environment.

Embracing implied tasks means deliberately welcoming a measured dose of controlled chaos into our plans and training, not as recklessness, but as a purposeful tool to expose leaders to the real variables, friction, and unpredictability they will face in any mission or problem. By intentionally creating space for ambiguity and adaptation during training, we compel junior leaders to think critically, prioritize under pressure, and exercise disciplined initiative. This is exactly how we build the agility and resilience that the National Guard demands when the plan inevitably collides with reality. If they fail, that's awesome! It's a win in a training environment. Let them learn from the mistakes that were made.

At its core, it's an investment in our people: the deliberate choice to develop adaptive, mission-focused professionals who can read the battlefield (or the emergency), understand the commander's intent, and act decisively without waiting for step-by-step guidance. When we trust our leaders to think, we stop building units that merely follow orders. We forge teams that anticipate, innovate, and win.

This shift from control to empowerment isn't easy. It requires mutual trust, shared understanding, and the courage to accept prudent risks. But it is precisely what doctrine (ADP 6-0) calls us to do, and it is what turns excellent Soldiers into exceptional leaders.

Let's choose development over micromanagement. When we do, the team doesn't just respond; the team prevails.

Leadership development in action

I assigned a junior Staff Sergeant to plan, resource, and execute a Claymore mine live-fire range. He had no prior experience with ranges of this scale, no background in explosives training coordination, and openly admitted he didn't know where to start. Rather than handing him a detailed checklist or walking him through every requirement, I gave him only the essentials: a key point of contact to reach out to first and a short list of probing questions designed to guide his thinking, questions like "What are the non-negotiable safety thresholds?" "How will you sequence the training to maximize repetitions?" and "What risks might emerge if weather or personnel change?" There were more probing questions, most of them we already discussed. Once he starting to see what was expected of him, he ran with it.

Then I stepped back. No daily oversight, no preemptive fixes, just a 90-day timeline with monthly concept briefings to the commander and me. This wasn't neglect; it was intentional space for him to identify and tackle the implied tasks himself: researching doctrine, coordinating ammunition and range facilities, building a safety plan, anticipating contingencies, and managing the human factors of a live explosive event.

Month by month, the briefings told the story. At first, his plan was rough and tentative. By the second briefing, he had consulted the subject matter experts (SMEs), identified friction points we hadn't mentioned, and started shaping a realistic timeline. By the third briefing, the concept was mature, detailed yet flexible, with clear risk mitigations and a focus on training value. We were quietly impressed by his progress, but we deliberately held back full praise. The real validation would come on execution day, not in the conference room.

When the range day arrived, he ran it flawlessly. Every requirement was covered: ammo accountability, crisp safety briefs, smooth Soldier flow, zero incidents, and maximum hands-on training for the entire unit. The once-daunting task of managing a live explosives range had been demystified. He handled variables, weather delays, Soldier fatigue, and last-minute adjustments with calm competence.

Afterward, I called him on the phone once the drill was over. His gratitude was genuine and unfiltered; he had learned more in those 90 days than in years of routine assignments. Most of all, he appreciated the trust we showed him, the unspoken belief that he could figure it out. That single vote of confidence built a level of self-assurance that no amount of classroom instruction or guided walkthrough could match.

I didn't give him a step-by-step, no implied tasks guide. He was given the conditions and environment to learn in, and that is exactly why he succeeded. By withholding the "how" and letting him develop his own implied tasks, It forced critical thinking, resourcefulness, and ownership. The trust we built was immeasurable—not just between us, but in his own judgment and in the unit's faith that NCOs can handle real responsibility.

This is the antidote to the implied task drought. Senior leaders must resist the urge to control every detail. Instead, set clear intent, provide minimal scaffolding, and create space for junior leaders to wrestle with ambiguity. In the National Guard, where civilian jobs compete for attention and missions can pivot overnight, this approach doesn't create chaos; it prepares people to master it. When we let NCOs go to work, we don't just complete tasks, we build leaders who think, adapt, and win.

Building the Framework to Support Team Development

One concept I never fully got to see in action, but often envisioned in theory, was a disciplined way for National Guard platoons to conduct Troop Leading Procedures (TLPs) despite the severe constraints of time. When you only have 39 training days a year to build a combat-ready unit, time management is not just important; it is decisive. It sounds unrealistic, almost reckless; to suggest you can build effective teams in that window. But it can be done, and I am convinced it starts with how leaders structure planning time.

The typical training days allocation in the National Guard is just 39 days: one weekend per month (usually two days, for a total of 24 days across 12 months) plus 15 days of annual training. That limited window is almost all part-time Soldiers get to build proficiency, cohesion, and readiness. Over time, making TLP routine produces confident platoon leadership, informed Soldiers, and teams that arrive at training ready to execute instead of scrambling to catch up.

The foundation of this framework begins with Army orders. Commanders must publish orders efficiently and on time. Handle battalion-level orders like hot potatoes: receive them, understand them, and immediately push them down. The company's responsibility is not to rewrite the battalion order, but to nest within the battalion commander's intent and translate it into clear, executable company-level guidance. The goal is simple: maximize platoon planning time.

If your commander cannot produce the order, guess who is stepping in to make sure it gets done? That's right, you are. Not to replace the commander, but to protect the unit. You help shape the order, organize the chaos, and ensure the formation has something clear to execute. That is not overstepping; this is meeting your higher commander's intent. I have seen peers at this level who have never written a company operations order. That should concern us. I again ask, how can a First Sergeant effectively advise a commander if they have never wrestled with building an order themselves? How can you refine a plan you've never constructed?

First Sergeants—learn to write orders. Build them. Struggle through them. The process sharpens your operational thinking and strengthens your ability to advise our young officers. If we expect to be the standard-bearers of readiness and discipline, we must also be students of planning and execution.

Ideally, the company operates on a 30-60-90 day planning model. Company orders are published 90 days out, giving platoons the time and mental space to digest the mission, identify friction points, and develop realistic plans. This timeline allows platoon leadership to move beyond reactive planning and into deliberate preparation, something Guard units rarely get the luxury to do.

Each month, the company conducts a training meeting no later than one week prior to the drill weekend. Timing matters. If the meeting happens too early, leaders forget the details. If it happens too late, there is no time to adjust. One week strikes a balance. During this meeting, platoons confirm their 30-day plan, back brief their 60-day plan, and begin developing their 90-day plan. The focus of this meeting remains firmly on the upcoming drill, the 30-day window, because that is where execution lives. We delve deeper into the 30-60-90 concept in the following chapter.

Once the drill weekend concludes and Soldiers return to the armory, the work does not stop. Platoons move into their planning bays and immediately begin refining the next 30-day plan. Squad leaders and Soldiers build terrain models, rehearse concepts, and prepare to brief their orders ahead of the next drill. Meanwhile, the commander is already shaping the next 90-day company order. This cycle repeats every drill weekend, creating a steady rhythm of planning, execution, and refinement.

If there is one term I have grown to hate, it is a "drill letter." A "drill letter" is a lazy substitute for planning, usually thrown together by a readiness NCO, reduced to the five W's, and disconnected from how units actually fight or train. It places responsibility on the wrong people and produces nothing of real value. The end state is not a drill letter; it is a fully developed Concept of Operations (CONOP) with the pertinent information squad leaders need to begin their necessary movement.

Every member of the platoon should receive the platoon's Concept of Operations (CONOP). It is owned by the platoon leadership, understood by the Soldiers, and shaped through repetition. When platoons operate this way, you are no longer just developing individual leaders; you are building teams. When teams have time, structure, and ownership, they become far more capable than any checklist or last-minute brief could ever make them.

This framework is not about perfection, and it is certainly not about adding more work to already compressed weekends. It is about discipline, ownership, and respecting the one resource the National Guard can never afford to waste: time. When leaders commit to publishing orders early, protecting platoon planning space, and forcing repetition through a predictable battle rhythm. Troop Leading Procedures stop being a theoretical concept and become a habit.

You might not recover all 39 days, but you can extract maximum value from them, and that's how I believe a part-time force builds formidable teams with limited training days.

Letting Go of Control

At its core, this entire framework is built around one simple idea: Letting go of control and **working yourself out of a job**, not in the sense of becoming irrelevant, but in the sense of becoming unnecessary at the point of execution. When leaders give platoons time, structure, and ownership, they no longer need to hover, correct, or rescue plans at the last minute. They have already done the work. You build trust.

Planning to work yourself out of a job means trusting subordinates with real responsibility, not rehearsed tasks, not scripted outcomes, but missions that require judgment and adaptation. It means accepting that they will not execute the plan exactly the way you would and understanding that mistakes drive development. The more a leader clings to control, the more fragile the organization becomes. The more they let go of control, the more resilient your teams grow.

When done right, the command team stops being the center of gravity for every decision and becomes the stabilizing force in the background. Platoons own their plans. Squads understand their purpose. Soldiers know what right looks like before the first formation ever happens. That is what it means to truly plan to work yourself out of a job.

Lessons in Action

I once led a squad on a deployment to the deserts of Iraq. When we finally arrived at our duty station in Baghdad, I had one clear goal: if things went sideways, my team would know exactly what to do without waiting on me. That meant rehearsals, relentless rehearsals. We trained until reactions became habits and habits became instinct. My boys would complain to me that the other squads were back in their living quarters playing video games. I remember my exact answer to them.

"I'll be goddammed if something happens and you don't know what to do!" I told them.

One of our primary challenges was vehicle recovery. We operated massive Mine-resistant Ambush Protected (MRAP) vehicles, and anyone who's dealt with them knows they are difficult to recover under ideal conditions, let alone under pressure. So, I turned the problem over to the team and added a little motivation. The section that could self-recover an MRAP the fastest would get the rest of the day off.

Here's something worth remembering, whether you're leading Soldiers or civilians: time and money are two of the biggest motivators out there. I couldn't give them more money, but I could give them time. That was enough.

The team took ownership of the problem in a way I never could have scripted. They studied the recovery process, experimented, and eventually designed a quick-release tow bar system that allowed them to hook up and recover a disabled

MRAP in roughly two minutes. I didn't direct the solution; I simply let them solve the problem.

Then, theory met reality.

While running a mission on Route Irish, one of the most notorious and treacherous routes in Iraq, one of our MRAPs broke down. Ironically, our mission that day was to deliver a recovery asset to another unit. Turns out we didn't need it.

Without hesitation, I called over the net, "Recovery, go!" The team sprang into action, set security, employed the quick-release system, aligned the vehicles, hooked up the tow bar, and we were moving again almost immediately. I didn't have a stopwatch, but if I had to guess, it was about a minute and a half. We recovered that truck without incident and kept rolling.

The real moment came during the post-mission After Action Review. The recovery asset team couldn't believe what they had seen. They openly admitted there was no way their team could have recovered that MRAP in that amount of time. The praise was unsolicited, genuine, and came from outside our organization.

That small validation lit a fire in my team.

From that point on, I never had to push rehearsals. The team drove training on their own. That was the moment I realized I had succeeded, not because I was in control, but because I no longer needed to be. They knew the standard, trusted each other, and executed without direction.

I only set the conditions. They did the rest.

Sometimes all a team needs is the space to own the problem, and a small spark of confirmation to realize just how capable they already are.

The Art of After-Action Review

I call it the **art** of the After Action Review because, at its best, an AAR is far more than asking a few standard questions or filling out a form. Like any art, it requires **judgment, timing, observation, and subtlety**. Two leaders can review the same training event and walk away with completely different outcomes depending on how they handle the discussion.

AARs are not mechanical, they are deeply human. They involve understanding people, reading the room, encouraging honesty, and knowing when to push for deeper insight or when to step back. Soldiers will not always volunteer the real issues unless they feel safe, respected, and heard. The art lies in creating an environment where they do.

Additionally, effective AARs require a balance between structure and flexibility. You need enough structure to ensure the discussion covers critical questions, what happened, why, and how to improve, but also the flexibility to explore unexpected insights. Some of the most valuable lessons come from observations no one anticipated: a small friction point in equipment use, a subtle communication failure, or a morale issue that only becomes visible in candid conversation.

Finally, AARs are an **art because they are about influence and culture**. A well-facilitated AAR shapes how Soldiers think about mistakes, ownership, and improvement. It transforms a single training event into lasting learning. Done poorly, it can demoralize, frustrate, or reinforce blame. Done well, it builds trust, empowers every member of the formation, and continuously improves the unit's performance.

In short, AARs are as much about **listening, observing, and connecting** as they are about recording facts. That combination of skill, intuition, and human understanding is what makes it an art.

The After Action Review (AAR) is one of the most powerful tools a leader has to improve performance, but only when it is conducted correctly. Too often AARs turn into casual conversations where people simply recount what happened, assign blame, and move on. When that happens, the opportunity to learn is lost.

A good AAR transforms experience into improvement. For that to happen, two things must be present: **deliberate facilitation and clear documentation.**

The Leader as Facilitator

During an AAR, the leader's role is not to dominate the conversation. The leader's role is to **facilitate it.**

A good facilitator guides the discussion so the team focuses on learning rather than personalities. The objective is simple: understand **what happened and why**.

Facilitating AARs is a skill that improves with practice. It can be difficult to manage in real time, especially when emotions run high after a challenging training event. But like any leadership skill, the more you practice it, the better you become.

Every AAR should revolve around a few core questions:

- What was the unit supposed to accomplish?

- What actually happened?

- Why was there a difference?

- What should we sustain?

- What should we improve before the next event?

These questions keep the discussion focused on learning instead of blame.

One of the most important aspects of a well-run AAR is ensuring that **everyone has the opportunity to contribute.** Junior Soldiers often see friction points that leaders miss. A driver, gunner, or team leader may identify a small problem that could become a major issue during real operations.

A well-facilitated AAR allows those observations to surface. The leader's responsibility is simply to keep the discussion **focused, constructive, and honest**.

If It Isn't Captured, It Is Lost

One of the most common failures in AARs is the lack of documentation.

Leaders talk through valuable lessons, everyone nods in agreement, and then the information disappears. When the next training event arrives, the same mistakes are repeated.

An effective AAR must produce a **clear record of observations and actions**.

Leaders should capture:

- What worked well

- What did not work

- Why the issue occurred

- What action will correct it

This documentation becomes a reference point for future training events. Over time it builds an institutional memory that prevents the unit from relearning the same lessons over and over again.

Capturing the Soldier's Perspective

One technique I found extremely effective was using a **simple digital survey** to collect feedback from Soldiers after major training events, particularly Annual Training.

Not every Soldier is comfortable speaking openly during a large group discussion. Rank dynamics, personalities, or simply the environment can prevent honest feedback. A short survey gives Soldiers another way to share what they experienced.

I used a basic Google Form to collect responses from across the formation. The survey was quick to complete and gave leaders valuable insight into how training was actually experienced at the Soldier level.

An added benefit was that the responses automatically populated into a spreadsheet. This allowed leaders to sort the feedback, review responses, and identify trends across the unit.

Using Data to Identify Trends

Once the survey data was collected, it could be exported into Excel where responses could be sorted, categorized, and reviewed.

Patterns began to appear when multiple Soldiers identified the same issue.

Several responses might highlight the same friction points—communication problems, unclear guidance, equipment shortages, or administrative frustrations. When the same comments begin appearing across multiple platoons or sections, leaders can quickly determine whether the issue is isolated or systemic.

Modern AI tools can also assist in reviewing survey responses by summarizing large amounts of written feedback and highlighting recurring themes. This allows leaders to quickly understand the overall concerns of the formation without manually sorting through every comment.

Technology does not replace leadership. But it can significantly improve a leader's ability to **capture lessons learned and turn feedback into action**.

Watching the Morale Indicator

One of the simplest questions on my survey became one of the most valuable:

"On a scale of 1–10, how would you rate company morale?"

I watched that number closely.

Over time, it became a quick indicator of how the company was feeling. When the responses began trending lower, it signaled that something beneath the surface needed attention.

Sometimes the issue was training fatigue. Sometimes it was administrative frustration. Other times it reflected the strain of balancing civilian life and military obligations in the Guard.

The number itself was not the answer. It simply pointed me toward where I needed to look.

When someone rated morale particularly low, I made a note of it. I did not always address it immediately, but when the right opportunity appeared—during a conversation in the motor pool, after drill, or during counseling—I would ask a simple question:

"Hey, I noticed you rated morale a little low on the survey. What's going on?"

That small question often opened the door to conversations that might never have happened otherwise. Sometimes the issue was minor and easily fixed. Other times it revealed deeper concerns that leadership needed to address.

Either way, that single question gave me an early look at the health of the company.

Example AAR Feedback Template

Below is a simple format that can be used to collect feedback after a major training event.

Basic Information

- Rank

- Platoon Assignment

- Full Name (for follow-up if required)

Mission Execution

- What was the Company/Platoon/Squad supposed to accomplish?

- Did the Company/Platoon/Squad accomplish the mission?

- What was the most valuable part of Annual Training?

- What aspects of training went well?

- How can we improve next time?

Leader Feedback

- What suggestions do you have for leadership?

Organizational Health

- On a scale of 1–10, how would you rate company morale?

Retention Indicators

- When do you ETS?

- Do you plan to extend?

- If not, why are you considering leaving?

Administrative Issues

- Do you currently have a pay problem?

- If yes, please provide details so leadership can assist.

Turning Feedback into Action

Collecting feedback only matters if it leads to improvement.

Leaders must review the information, identify recurring themes, and turn those observations into training adjustments or process improvements. Just as importantly, Soldiers must see that their feedback actually matters.

During one survey, a Soldier pointed out something simple but frustrating: our armory did not have enough mop buckets to properly clean the building after training. It was not a major operational issue, but it was a real friction point for the Soldiers responsible for maintaining the facility.

The comment could have easily been ignored. Instead, we addressed it.

By the next drill weekend, we had purchased additional mop buckets and cleaning supplies. It was a small fix, but when Soldiers saw the new equipment sitting in the supply room, it sent a clear message: **their feedback had been heard and acted upon.**

That moment reinforced something important across the formation. The surveys were not just another administrative requirement. They were a way for Soldiers to improve their environment and their unit.

Small problems often have small solutions. But when leaders consistently act on feedback, it builds trust within the formation and encourages Soldiers to continue speaking honestly about what needs to improve.

Over time those small improvements add up. They create a culture where the unit is constantly identifying problems, solving them, and getting better.

And that is the real purpose of an After-Action Review: **to ensure the team is better tomorrow than it was today.**

Wrapping It Up

This chapter was never about training schedules, ranges, or planning models. Those are just tools. The real lesson is about trust, restraint, and intentional leadership. Teams do not grow because senior leaders do all the planning or provide step-by-step instructions. They grow because leaders will let go of control at the right moments and accept short-term discomfort for long-term competence.

When you empower others with real responsibility, responsibility that carries consequences, you send a clear message: *I trust you to think, to plan, and to execute.* That trust changes behavior. It turns rehearsals into habits, planning into ownership, and Soldiers into professionals who do not wait to be told what to do when pressure arrives.

Planning to work yourself out of a job does not make you less relevant; it strengthens your organization. At its core, it just deliberate succession of command. This guarantees that when chaos arises, decisions won't be held up by those at the top. Leaders at the lowest capable level decide on what actions to take at the decision point. Trust your NCOs and allow them space to lead missions.

The art of the After-Action Review lies in turning experience into learning. It is not just about asking questions or recording observations, it is about listening, guiding, and creating an environment where every Soldier can share insights. When conducted thoughtfully, an AAR captures lessons, identifies trends, strengthens trust, and improves both individual and unit performance. In short, it ensures the team is better and continues to improve. Please remember to document the lessons and have a plan to put them into action.

Chapter Six

Communication

The Hardest Simple Thing We Do

> "If I could turn an Army Operations Order into a 15-second reel on social media, I'd have solved all communication issues in the Army!"

I f you have ever sat through an after-action review in the military, you can almost guarantee that communication will show up somewhere on the whiteboard. It might be written as *"need clearer guidance," "better dissemination,"* or the classic catch-all, *"communications breakdown."* No matter the mission, the environment, or the echelon, communication is almost always identified as something that needs improvement.

That pattern isn't accidental. In my experience, roughly 90% of leadership failures can be traced back to communication as the primary culprit. Not lack of effort. Not lack of competence. Not even a lack of resources. People were willing. The plan existed. The intention was good. But somewhere between thought and execution, the message degraded.

So why is communication so difficult? And why, after decades of doctrine, training, and technology, are we still trying to get better at it?

The problem is that communication is often treated as a simple problem to solve, when in reality it is anything but. We confuse talking with real communicating. Just because something was said, briefed, emailed, or written doesn't mean it was understood. Too often, leaders assume their job is done once the information leaves their mouth or appears on a slide. In truth, that is just the starting point, the hard work of ensuring understanding begins the moment the message is sent.

Communication is not a one-time act; it must be a system. It requires repetition, confirmation, and reinforcement. Messages decay as they move down the chain. Stress, fatigue, assumptions, and competing priorities can distort messages. What makes perfect sense to a commander or first sergeant in a planning session may be confusing, incomplete, or misinterpreted by the time it reaches a squad at midnight in the rain.

Another reason communication fails is that leaders often overestimate clarity and underestimate the friction involved. Often we plan in clean rooms with whiteboards, air conditioning, and coffee. Execution occurs amid noise, darkness, weather, and pressure. The more complex the plan, the more fragile communication becomes. When things go wrong, and they always do, unclear intent and poorly communicated priorities are exposed immediately.

There is also a human factor we rarely acknowledge: people hear what they *expect* to hear. Rank, experience, and organizational culture all shape how messages are received. Subordinates may hesitate to ask clarifying questions. Leaders may assume silence equals understanding. Neither is true. Silence often means confusion, not comprehension.

Finally, communication is hard because it requires discipline and humility. It demands that leaders slow down, listen, and verify understanding, not just issue direction. It requires accepting that if a message was misunderstood, the failure belongs to the sender, not the receiver. That is an uncomfortable truth for many leaders, but it is a necessary one.

This chapter is not about sending messages over the radio, PowerPoint slides, or clever briefing techniques. It is about communication as a leadership responsibility. It is about how intent is shared, how trust is built, and how teams function under stress. Because when communication is clear, simple, and deliberate, friction decreases, initiative increases, and leaders at every level are empowered to act.

I will not pretend that I have solved the communication problem. In truth, I don't think anyone ever has. I consider myself a student of communication, not a master; I am still learning, still making mistakes, and remain a novice in many respects. What follows is not a list of perfect answers, but lessons learned through trial, failure, and reflection, shared in the hope that they help you shorten your own learning curve.

Understanding Communication

The Army defines communication as a critical process that involves the clear transmission of messages, fostering shared understanding, and facilitating effective leadership and operations[7]. Cool. That sounds great in doctrine, but doctrine doesn't lead Soldiers. Leaders do. So let's break this down into what it actually means for a senior leader.

Communication extends far beyond the words you speak. Whether you intend it or not, you are always communicating. Every action, or deliberate lack of action, sends a message. Right now, as you read this book, you are communicating something: you are investing time in growth and self-improvement. To those around you, your Soldiers, your peers, your family, that simple act loudly declares you are a lifelong learner, even if that's not the message you consciously set out to send. It is received clearly, nevertheless. The same principle applies in uniform: the way you carry yourself, the condition of your gear, or even how you stand during a company formation speaks volumes before you ever open your mouth.

When you arrive early, you demonstrate your commitment to standards. When you show up late, you communicate priorities. Acceptance is communicated when you walk past a deficiency. When you only speak up when something is wrong, you communicate fear instead of trust. Soldiers are constantly reading the room, and senior leaders are the loudest voice in it, even when they are silent.

For senior leaders, communication breaks down into a few practical realities:

Presence communicates intent.

Where you spend your time tells your outfit what matters. If you are always in the office, you are telling leaders that paperwork matters more than people. If you are routinely in the field or the training area, you communicate that readiness matters. Presence is not micromanagement, it is emphasis. There is a limit though, try not to over "presence" your welcome. Let the team get to work.

Consistency communicates credibility.

If what you say in formation does not match what you tolerate behind closed doors, Soldiers will believe your actions, not your words. Senior leaders lose credibility not because they make mistakes, but because they are inconsistent. Standards enforced sometimes are standards that don't exist.

Silence communicates approval.

This one hurts because it's usually unintentional. When a leader fails to correct something, especially something small, it sends a powerful message: *this is acceptable now.* Senior leaders don't need to correct everything, but they must be deliberate about what they ignore, because your Soldiers are keeping score.

Tone communicates priority.

How you say something matters just as much as what you say. If every conversation sounds like a crisis, your team will burn out. If you are calm when things go wrong and intense when standards slip, you communicate maturity and focus. Leaders set the emotional climate, whether or not they mean to.

The key takeaway is this: communication is not an event, a briefing, or an order, it is a constant condition or a system. Senior leaders don't turn communication on and off. They live inside it. Once you accept that reality, you stop asking, *"Did I say it?"* and start asking the only question that matters:

"What message did my Soldiers receive? What actions will result?"

The receiver always gets a vote in how your message lands. Communication is tough because it's inherently subjective—what you say, what they hear, and what they remember are almost never the same thing. Every word gets filtered through their experiences, personality, stress level, and perspective.

Leaders often think they've been crystal clear because the message made perfect sense in their own heads. But the team is hearing it through their own reality, and those two realities rarely line up.

When a gap shows, our knee-jerk fix is usually more policy, more procedures, more binders, hoping clarity on paper will magically fix confusion in practice. Truth is, Soldiers don't read your stuff. In my experience, they only crack open regs or written guidance when they're trying to dodge something or they're already in hot water.

Communication needs a real strategy, an attack plan. Hit them from every angle: announce it loud in your formation, write it down clearly, blast it out in an email, via text, or group chat. You can continuously hammer it home in one-on-ones. People absorb information differently, some need to hear it, some need to read it, and some need it face-to-face. Stick to one channel, and you're deliberately leaving part of your formation in the dark. Intentional redundancy isn't overkill; it's a communication system. Consistent multi-lane messaging kills confusion, kills assumptions, and gets the team moving fast, with no one wasting time decoding what "leadership intent" really means.

Realities of Creating Shared Understanding

I can think of two examples of a common language that allow people from any culture, background, or experience level to come together and complete complex tasks with little to no prior coordination: sheet music and, strangely enough, LEGO instruction booklets. Both rely on standardized systems that create a shared foundation before any action begins. That standardization makes shared understanding possible.

Music works because it follows an agreed-upon language structure. Time signatures, tempo, keys, and notation form a universal language that musicians learn long before they ever play together. Because that language is standardized, a group of strangers can sit down, open sheet music, and perform as a unit. They do not need constant verbal direction because they share an understanding of how the system works and where the music is supposed to go. Even when mistakes happen, the structure allows the group to adjust and recover without stopping.

LEGO instruction booklets function similarly. They use a standardized visual language, symbols, steps, orientation, and sequencing that require no written explanation. A child in the United States and an adult in another country can open the same box and build the same structure because the instructions establish a common reference point. The standard removes ambiguity and reduces interpretation, allowing individuals to focus on execution instead of guessing intent. The front of the Lego box clearly states the intent.

These standards enable a shared understanding. They do not tell people how to think; they give them a common framework to think within. Once that framework exists, coordination becomes easier, adaptation becomes faster, and trust in the process increases.

Organizations are no different. Shared understanding does not happen by accident, and it does not emerge simply because information was pushed out. It must be built on common standards, language, expectations, processes, and definitions of success. When those standards are clear, leaders can communicate intent once and trust their teams to act within it.

In military formations, this allows decentralized execution to work. When Soldiers understand the standard and the intent, they can make decisions in real time without waiting for further guidance. Orders stop being scripts and become references. Leaders stop micromanaging and start enabling.

Music and LEGO instructions work because they establish standards before execution ever begins. That is exactly the role Standard Operating Procedures (SOPs) are supposed to play in an organization. SOPs create a common language, a baseline understanding of how things are done, so leaders do not have to explain the fundamentals every time a task arises.

SOPs can answer the "how." Intent answers the "why."

Too often, leaders confuse these two or misuse one to compensate for the other. When SOPs are weak or nonexistent, leaders try to compensate by issuing overly detailed orders. When intent is unclear, leaders hide behind SOPs and expect blind compliance. Both approaches can fail, just in different ways.

SOPs should function like sheet music. They establish rhythm, tempo, and structure so that execution can occur smoothly without constant direction. When SOPs are well understood, leaders do not need to micromanage routine actions. Soldiers already know how to clear a room, conduct pre-combat checks and inspections (PCCs/PCIs), execute a recovery, or run a range. That cognitive load is removed from the moment of execution.

Intent, on the other hand, is what allows adaptation when the situation changes. Intent gives meaning to the SOP. It explains what success looks like and what matters most when things go wrong. Without intent, SOPs become rigid checklists that break the moment reality deviates from the plan. Without SOPs, intent becomes abstract and execution becomes chaotic.

Shared understanding exists at the intersection of SOPs and intent. Soldiers who understand both can operate independently while still moving in the same direction. They know what must be done, how it is normally done, and, most importantly, what to prioritize when the plan no longer fits the problem.

Therefore, leaders must resist the urge to over-communicate tactics and under-communicate their intent. If leaders spend all their time explaining how to do something that should already be standardized, they rob their teams of the ability to think. Conversely, if they only communicate intent without establishing common procedures, they set the conditions for misalignment and frustration.

Effective communication means investing time upfront to build strong SOPs and then consistently reinforcing intent. When that foundation exists, leaders can say less and achieve more. Orders become shorter. Briefings become clearer. Execution becomes faster.

Just as musicians can improvise because they understand the structure of the music, Soldiers can adapt because they understand both the SOP and the intent behind it. That is not accidental; it results from disciplined leadership and deliberate communication.

Communications in Action

We have spent some time discussing what communication is and unpacking the theory behind it. That matters, but theory without application does nothing for your outfit. This section is about action. The goal is to give you a practical starting point to build a communications foundation and, ultimately, a communications SOP for your organization.

To improve communication, you must design systems that ensure it occurs consistently, rather than relying on individual motivation or memory.

Start with your battle rhythm.

In my continuity book (a handover document every good leader prepares for their replacement capturing key processes, contacts, and hard-won lessons), I wrote that the battle rhythm is the beating heart of an organization. If it becomes irregular or collapses, everything else can fail: information stops flowing, decisions get delayed, and confusion fills the gaps. You must fight to establish it, protect it, and maintain its consistency.

Your battle rhythm should be the first pillar of your communications SOP.

A disciplined battle rhythm does more than schedule meetings; it creates predictable moments where information is shared, decisions are made, and intent is reinforced. When leaders know when communication will occur, they spend less time gathering information and more time preparing to act on it. Predictability reduces friction and builds trust.

Once established, the battle rhythm must be treated as sacred. Canceling or constantly shifting events sends a message that communication is optional. It suggests that reacting is more important than planning. Over time, that mindset erodes shared understanding. Change in your battle rhythm will be inevitable, but approach it deliberately and understand the effects it will have on your subordinates. Sometimes a seemingly simple change at your level can end up creating a tsunami event at your subordinate level.

A strong battle rhythm also allows leaders to communicate less, not more. When teams know that guidance, feedback, and decisions will happen at known intervals, leaders do not need to push information haphazardly through texts, emails, and last-minute briefings. The system carries the message. The team knows what to prepare for prior to each event. This predictability ends up buying you time to lead.

If communication is failing in your organization, do not start by talking louder or sending more emails. Start by examining your battle rhythm. If the heartbeat is weak or inconsistent, no amount of messaging will fix it.

Set the rhythm. Protect it. Build everything else on top of it.

Examples of Battle Rhythms

Below is a practical, realistic battle rhythm for a National Guard Infantry Company that drills one weekend a month, with Annual Training (AT) as the culminating event. This is written for leaders who live in the real world, have limited time, civilian jobs, and zero tolerance for wasted drill hours.

These battle rhythms protect planning time, build shared understanding, and deliberately prepare platoons for AT, not just to survive each drill. Remember what we learned from the last chapter, your primary deliverable to your team is your platoon CONOP, not a dang drill letter, this method ensures your platoon leadership takes ownership of their plans so they are not dependent on you to lead their teams.

National Guard Infantry Company Battle Rhythm

Built on a 30–60–90 Planning Model

Purpose: Deliberately build readiness over time and arrive at Annual Training prepared to execute—not improvise.

When time is limited, predictability becomes a combat multiplier. A disciplined 30–60–90 planning model gives platoons the time and clarity they need to plan, rehearse, and execute effectively. For a National Guard infantry company, this structure transforms monthly drills from isolated events into a connected progression toward Annual Training (AT).

The 30–60–90 Framework (What it Means)

90 Days Out: Company publishes intent and broad guidance.

60 Days Out: Platoons refine concepts and identify friction.

30 Days Out: Finalize execution details and rehearse.

Drill Weekend: Execute, assess, and adjust.

Each month, platoons execute **the 30-day plan**, **refine the 60-day plan**, and **shape the 90-day plan** simultaneously.

The 90-Day Window (Planning Foundation)

Focus: Establish intent and give platoons time to think.

Battalion order received and immediately pushed down.

The company publishes its order nested in the Battalion's intent.

The commander clearly articulates the purpose and end state.

Platoons begin initial mission analysis.

Key resourcing and logistical friction points identified early.

Outcome: Platoon leadership understands *where the unit is going*, even if all the details are not yet finalized.

The 60-Day Window (Planning Refinement)

Focus: Turn intent into executable concepts.

Platoons refine their CONOPs.

Squad leaders are brought into the planning process.

Leaders identify risks, resourcing shortfalls, and timeline conflicts.

Adjustments made before they become drill-day surprises.

Outcome: Platoons are no longer reacting; they are shaping the mission.

The 30-Day Window (Plan Confirmation)

Focus: Lock in execution and validate shared understanding.

Company Training Meeting (NO LATER THAN ONE WEEK PRIOR TO DRILL).

This meeting is non-negotiable. Conducted **at least one week prior to the drill weekend.**

Primary purpose:

Verify the plan.

Validate shared understanding.

Identify last-minute friction points.

Platoons will:

Confirm the 30-day plan (upcoming drill).

Backbrief their 60-day plan.

Brief initial concepts for their 90-day plan.

Command Team will:

Ensure the intent is clearly understood.

Confirm logistics, transportation, and resourcing.

Resolve conflicts while there is still time to fix them.

Why one-week matters:

Too early, and details are forgotten.

Too late, and leaders have no time to react.

One week is the sweet spot.

Drill Weekend—Execution (The 30-Day Plan Realized)

Purpose: Execute what was planned, with no surprises for you or your team.

Day 1—Orientation & Alignment:

Accountability and admin.

Commander's intent (reiterated).

Platoon orders or FRAGOs.

Rehearsals and walk-throughs.

Movement to training site.

Initiate Training event.

Day 2—Training and Repetition:

Squad and platoon collective training.

STX lanes, ranges, or patrols.

Leaders observe, coach, and assess.

Day 2.5—Integration and Stress

Reduced guidance.

Added friction.

Platoons operate using intent and SOPs.

Day 3—Movement Back and Recovery

Close out all training events.

movement back to home stations.

Last Day of Drill Weekend—Transition to the Next Training Cycle

Immediately after training and your unit returns to home station:

Platoons return to the planning bay.

The next 30-day plan begins development.

Squad leaders and Soldiers continue refining concepts.

Leaders complete their administrative tasks.

Command Team:

Commander shapes the next 90-day order.

First Sergeant enforces discipline in the battle rhythm.

Logistics gaps are addressed while lessons are fresh.

End-of-drill AAR:

Honest assessment.

Lessons tied directly to upcoming Annual Training.

Identify SOP updates and planning adjustments.

This cycle repeats every month.

The End-State: Platoons are Ready for Annual Training.

By the time Annual Training arrives,

Platoons have already executed pieces of AT multiple times.

Leaders are confident, not reactive.

SOPs are tested and owned.

Soldiers understand the mission before the first formation.

AT becomes a **validation event**, not a learning curve.

Why This Model Works?

It protects planning time.

It creates a shared understanding.

It forces repetition.

It reduces friction before it matters.

Most importantly, it allows leaders to **plan themselves out of a job** by giving platoons the time, structure, and ownership required to lead.

When planning is deliberate and predictable, execution becomes decisive—even in a part-time force.

Active Duty Garrison Week

Now, I would be remiss if I did not include an active-duty battle rhythm example for my active-duty brethren. What follows is a practical, senior-leader–friendly weekly battle rhythm for a typical garrison work week. This is not a theoretical construct or a doctrinal template. It supports communication, builds shared understanding, and enables disciplined execution without drowning the organization in meetings.

The purpose of a battle rhythm is not to fill calendars. It is to create predictability, protect leader time, and ensure that decisions are made at the right level, at the right time, and with the right people present. Active-Duty Example Weekly Battle Rhythm (Monday–Friday)

Monday—Direction and Alignment

Purpose: Set priorities, confirm intent, and align leaders for the week.

05:00–07:00 | Physical Fitness

08:00–08:30 | Command Team Sync

Commander, First Sergeant, XO

Review the commander's priorities.

Identify friction points from last week.

Confirm decision authority and messaging.

09:00–10:00 | Leader Huddle

Platoon leaders, platoon sergeants, key staff

Commander's intent for the week.

Top 3 priorities (no more).

Constraints and decision points.

Key events or risks.

1300–1400 | Maintenance / Admin Update

Status of equipment, personnel, and readiness drivers.

Focus on issues that affect execution *this week*.

Why it matters: Monday answers *"What matters this week?"* If leaders leave unclear, the rest of the week is wasted.

Tuesday—Planning and Preparation

Purpose: Turn intent into executable plans.

05:00–07:00 | Physical Fitness

09:00–11:00 | Planning Window (Protected Time)

Platoons and sections plan.

No taskings, no interruptions.

Leaders develop CONOPs, schedules, and resourcing.

1300–1500 | Backbriefs (as needed)

Platoons' brief upcoming training or missions.

Focus on *how* they plan to execute the commander's intent.

The command team listens more than talks.

Why it matters: This is where shared understanding is built. Leaders learn how their subordinates think.

Wednesday—Execution and Assessment

Purpose: Execute and assess in real time.

05:00–07:00 | Physical Fitness

08:00–08:30 | Midweek Check

Quick sync (standing meeting).

What's working?

What's broken?

Do we need to adjust priorities?

Remainder of Day | Training / Operations

Leaders are present.

Observe; don't interfere.

Capture observations for feedback.

Why it matters: Midweek corrections prevent Friday surprises.

Thursday—Refinement and Development

Purpose: Improve performance and develop leaders.

05:00–07:00 | Physical Fitness

09:00–10:00 | After Action Reviews (AARs)

Focus on 2–3 key lessons.

Tie the observations back to the intent.

Capture adjustments for the next iteration.

1300–1430 | Leader Development / NCO Professional Development

Case studies.

Planning exercises.

Rehearsals for upcoming events.

No PowerPoint unless absolutely necessary.

Why it matters: This is where experience turns into learning.

Friday—Closure and Communication

Purpose: Close the loop and set conditions for next week.

05:00–07:00 | Physical Fitness

08:00–08:30 | Weekly Closeout

What did we accomplish?

What carries over?

What does "good" look like next week?

1000–1130 | Admin / Soldier Care

Leave, pay, family issues.

Leader presence matters here.

1500 | Release Formation

Clear guidance.

No last-minute taskings.

Respect time.

Why it matters: How you end the week shapes morale and trust.

Key Principles Behind This Battle Rhythm:

Predictability beats volume.

Meetings have a purpose, not a habit.

Protected planning time is non-negotiable.

The intent is reinforced multiple times, not once.

Leaders talk less and listen more.

These examples of battle rhythms are your **communications SOP in action**. When maintained, it reduces chaos, builds shared understanding, and allows leaders to **work themselves out of a job**.

Remember, these examples are only a foundational approach to establishing how your organization communicates. It is not the final answer, and it is not meant to be rigid. Think of it as the framework upon which everything else is built. The main goal of this is to establish a shared understanding.

Once the battle rhythm is set, leaders can go deeper and deliberately decide *how* messages move through the organization. This is where communication methods and primary, alternate, contingent, and emergent (PACE) planning come into play. Leaders must determine when email is appropriate, when a phone call is required, when a text message is sufficient, and when the situation demands the oldest method of all: sending a runner.

PACE plans are not just for tactical operations; they apply equally to garrison and training environments. If email fails, what's next? If phones are down, how does information still flow? If digital tools create confusion instead of clarity, how do leaders reestablish control?

The point is not to overcomplicate communication, but to be intentional about it. When leaders deliberately design how information moves—rather than reacting when it breaks—they reduce friction, preserve shared understanding, and keep the organization moving forward, even when conditions change.

This is how communication stops being a constant problem and starts becoming a combat multiplier.

Wrapping It Up

Now, I know we didn't solve all the communication problems, in fact, we barely scratched the surface, but at least we've established a starting point for your senior leader role. The goal here isn't perfection; it's to give you a framework to build from. You now have the tools to define a battle rhythm, set expectations, create shared understanding, and plan for multiple ways to transmit information when things inevitably go sideways.

Remember, communication is not a one-way street. It is a living, iterative process that requires attention, patience, and constant reinforcement. The methods, meetings, and messages we've discussed are just the beginning. How you tailor them to your team, your unit, and your mission is where the real work—and real impact—happens.

If there is one takeaway to leave this section with, it's this: communication is never "done." Your success as a senior leader is measured not by how much you talk or how many slides you present, but by how well your team understands, executes, and adapts. Establish the foundation, reinforce it relentlessly, and over time, you will build a unit where intent is clear, understanding is shared, and execution becomes second nature.

We set out to tackle the thing that shows up on every whiteboard after every mission: communication. We've unpacked why it's the hardest simple thing leaders do, messages decay, humans filter through their own realities, friction turns clear plans into confusion, and silence often hides misunderstanding rather than agreement. We've redefined it not as an event or a briefing, but as a constant condition: presence, consistency, tone, and every action (or inaction) sending signals Soldiers read louder than words.

We explored how shared understanding doesn't happen by accident. It's built on common frameworks, like sheet music for musicians or LEGO instructions for builders, translated into military terms as strong SOPs for the "how" and crystal-clear commander's intent for the "why." When those two intersect, teams stop waiting for direction and start executing with initiative, even when the plan inevitably changes.

Your success as a senior leader isn't measured by how many slides you briefed or how loudly you spoke. It's measured by how well your team understands the mission, adapts when friction hits, and moves as one toward the objective. Do the deliberate work upfront, reinforce it daily, and over time you'll build a unit where intent is shared, trust is earned, and execution feels instinctive.

Communication will still show up on the next AAR whiteboard. That's okay. The difference is that now you'll know why—and you'll have the tools to make it better. Keep learning. Keep listening. Keep owning the message.

Because in the end, clear communication isn't just leadership; it's how leaders win, how teams win, and how you can take will action to make your organization better!

Chapter Seven

The Standard Bearer

Buying Freedom Through Discipline

> "Discipline is the soul of an army. It makes small numbers formidable; procures success to the weak, and esteem to all." — George Washington.

There is an all-too-familiar joke in the Army: when you graduate from the Sergeant Major Academy, they hand you your diploma in one hand and your official "pet peeve" in the other. It might be grooming standards, walking on grass, or the sacredness of the greeting of the day. I remember swearing to myself, loudly and repeatedly, that I would **not** become "the uniform guy." I was going to be the cool, mission-focused First Sergeant who didn't sweat the small stuff. The standards would take care of themselves, right?

Wrong.

My Soldiers made sure of that.

Those beautiful, stubborn, gloriously defiant jerks tested my resolve every day. They'd show up with helmets with no covers, Soldier of Fortune boots, reflective-lens sunglasses, or patches sewn on with the creative liberty that would make a seamstress weep. The list can go on and on. It wasn't malice; it was just the natural entropy of a part-time force, civilian jobs, family demands, late-night drives, and the occasional "eh, close enough" moment.

I explained, multiple times, patiently at first, then with increasing clarity, that if they wanted to be **special** and wear something different, we already have an entire organization in the Army whose first name is "Special." They can go try out for the Green Berets anytime. Until then, we're not them. We're an infantry company. A cohesive team. We look like one. We act as one. We fight as one.

Look at the **All Blacks**, New Zealand's legendary national rugby team. They don't show up in mismatched jerseys, custom sleeves, or personal flair, everything is strictly uniform, from the iconic all-black kit with the silver fern to the coordinated shoes and shorts. The team uniform is non-negotiable because it signals unity, professionalism, and a shared purpose. When the All Blacks step onto the field, often after performing the powerful haka, everyone knows exactly who they are: a collective force representing an entire nation. The same principle applies in the military. A sharp, matching uniform isn't vanity, it's identity. It tells every Soldier, every leader, every outsider: "This is who we are. We do things the right way, every time."

Quick note: The All Blacks famously treat their black jersey as sacred: players are custodians rather than owners, there are no individual names on the back during matches to emphasize team over self, and the design has stayed remarkably consistent for over a century to honor legacy and collective pride, not individuals. Sometimes even those serving in the United States Armed Forces need a simple reminder of why we wear the uniform and who we represent.

So, despite my best efforts and loud internal protests, I was forced to become **the uniform guy**.

In the National Guard, where time is precious, the uniform isn't just clothing; it's the most visibly loud signal of discipline, attention to detail, and shared identity.

When your formation looks sharp, it quietly announces: "We can get the small things right, so you can trust us with the big things when it counts."

Flip that picture around: if your company looks like a wild, disorganized pack of hooligans with no uniformity, mismatched gear, and zero cohesion, you can be damn sure your bosses are going to look deeper. And they won't have to dig far to find the problem.

That problem is usually you.

Remember the hard lessons about communication from Chapter 5: appearance is non-verbal communication at its loudest. A sloppy formation is clear evidence that something is broken in the culture, the standards, or the leadership. You don't need to be "the uniform guy" to enforce it, but you do need to be the leader who refuses to let "good enough" become the standard. When the uniform is right, the message is clear: this unit is ready, this unit is professional, and this unit is led by quality leadership.

I still don't want to be "the uniform guy." I'd much rather pour my energy into building better training plans, creating realistic scenarios, or fostering a true warrior culture to get measurable results on readiness. But the battle for uniform standards is one that will never be won. It's a fight that must be fought constantly. Let it slide even a little, and the small cracks become canyons: mismatched uniforms turn into mismatched expectations, unauthorized boots become unauthorized standards, and before you know it, the whole formation looks like it's operating on "good enough."

So let's set the conditions to buy back your freedom to lead through discipline.

Discipline Equals Freedom

Discipline is frequently misunderstood as punishment, the corrective action that comes after someone screws up. And don't get me wrong: I've spent plenty of hours on extra duty because I was a young Soldier who needed to learn the hard way. That kind of discipline was exactly the medicine I required at the time; it curbed my ego, taught me consequences, and forced me to think before I spoke again. But here's the key distinction: punishment is reactive, a response to failure after it's already happened. True discipline is proactive structure, the daily framework you build upfront to make failure the exception, not the rule.

Think of it like this: punishment is the ER visit after you crash your vehicle; discipline is the pre-trip inspection, the practiced maneuvers, and the guardrails that keep you from wrecking in the first place. In my early days as a young NCO, those extra duties were necessary course corrections, they stung, but they worked because someone enforced standards consistently. As a senior leader, though, I shifted my focus: why wait for the crash? In the Guard, with our limited training windows, reactive punishment drains time we can't afford. Proactive discipline saves it. Proactive discipline can also save lives.

You are the standard-bearer, you set the tone, you enforce the structure, you model what right looks like every single day. But you are also human, and humans are imperfect. Fatigue creeps in after a 60-hour work week. Ego flares when a junior leader pushes back on your plan. Complacency whispers that "we can skip the last formation today" or "one missed backbrief won't hurt." Those are the exact moments when discipline stops being something you impose on others and becomes the armor you wear to protect your own integrity, and the units.

The systems you build, the battle rhythm you fight to protect, the first and last formations you refuse to cancel, the tiered training ownership you delegate but still oversee, the Shoot-Move-Communicate checklists you run before every major event, are not just for the formation. They are guardrails for **you**. They keep you from drifting into rationalizations, from cutting corners when no one is watching, from becoming the leader who preaches accountability but tolerates exceptions for himself. Discipline protects your credibility when your willpower alone isn't enough.

Sometimes I was mentally checked out, family stress, deadlines, sleep deprivation, and the easy path was to let things slide. "It's just one weekend." "They'll figure it out." But you have to fight to not give in to that temptation, the formation senses it immediately. Standards eroded fast if you let them. It is not an easy battle; you will have to come to terms with that. There is no easy button for establishing your own discipline. If you begin to falter, just fall back on your systems or battle rhythm to reevaluate your azimuth.

I forced discipline into my own routines as fiercely as I forced it into the unit's. I showed up early for every first formation, even when I wanted to crawl back into bed. I ended every drill with a final formation, even when all I wanted was to go home. I ran my own mental shoot-move-communicate checks before major decisions, even when no one else was looking. Those minor acts of self-discipline weren't glamorous. They weren't noticed by most people. But they protected me from ego, from burnout, from becoming the hypocritical leader I swore I'd never be. They kept me honest. They kept the unit honest.

As the senior leader, your greatest responsibility isn't just to the formation, it's to the version of yourself you want to be remembered as. Discipline is the armor that protects that version of yourself from your own very human flaws. Embrace it. Fight for it relentlessly. Because when you protect yourself with discipline, you protect everyone who follows you.

That's how discipline truly equals freedom, not just for the team, but for you as well.

Wrapping It Up: Carry the Standard

This chapter is about **ownership**. About accepting the uncomfortable truth that standards don't drift on their own—*they drift because leaders allow them to.* And once you accept that, you also accept the weight and privilege of being the standard-bearer.

As the senior leader, you don't get the luxury of selective discipline. You don't get to enforce standards only when it's convenient, visible, or interesting. The formation will forgive many mistakes, bad calls, even moments of uncertainty—but they will never forgive inconsistency and poor leadership. Every time you let something slide, you quietly teach them what really matters. Every time you enforce a standard, especially when it's inconvenient, you reinforce trust.

Being the standard-bearer means understanding that discipline is not about control—it's about clarity. It removes friction. It reduces uncertainty. It frees your leaders and Soldiers to focus on the mission instead of guessing where the line is today. When standards are clear and consistently enforced, your organization moves faster, trains harder, and adapts better under stress. That is freedom in its purest form.

You don't carry the standard because you enjoy correcting people. You carry it because someone has to. Because units without standards don't suddenly rise to the occasion when things get hard—they fracture. Because when the first round cracks overhead, no one wishes they had been more relaxed about discipline in garrison.

So carry it with humility. Carry it with consistency. Carry it even when you're tired, frustrated, or ready to move on. Because long after your change-of-responsibility inventory is signed and your guidon has passed to the next leader, the culture you enforced—or failed to—will still be standing in formation.

And whether they stand sharp or sloppy will tell everyone exactly what kind of leader you were. So be sharp!

Chapter Eight

Unlimited Potential

The Danger of Early Labels

> "Why would I want to judge somebody today when I don't know who's going to turn out to be great in the future?" — Edwards Deming

One of the most dangerous habits leaders develop is believing they can predict the future. We label Soldiers early, high performer, average, problem child, future NCO, lost cause, and then spend the rest of our time reinforcing those assumptions. Promotions, opportunities, patience, and mentorship often follow the label instead of the potential. The truth is: **we are terrible at forecasting who will be great, and that is okay.**

What makes early labeling so dangerous is not just that it limits opportunity; it quietly shapes identity. When a young Soldier is repeatedly treated as a "problem," they begin to internalize that narrative. Confidence erodes, initiative fades, and eventually they become the label you assigned them.

On the other hand, when someone is prematurely labeled a "star," they can become afraid to fail, protecting reputation instead of pursuing development. Or worse, they become entitled and resistant to growth. Labels create ceilings and cages. They narrow a person's view of who they can become long before their potential has had time to unfold.

Every senior leader can point to someone they once underestimated who later became exceptional. We can all think of someone who looked like a sure thing and quietly plateaued or was an epic failure. Talent is not linear. Growth is not predictable. People mature at different speeds, under different pressures, and often in ways no counseling statement or NCOER could ever capture in the moment.

Standards still matter. Accountability still matters. But leadership at the senior level is less about identifying the next star and more about **building an environment where stars are allowed to emerge**. You do not create greatness by selecting it, you create it by cultivating it.

Your actual job is not to judge who will succeed. Your job is to **design a culture that gives everyone a fair chance to grow**, fail, learn, and try again. When the culture is right—when discipline is consistent, communication is clear, development is intentional, and trust is real—people tend to rise to the level of expectation placed on them. Some will surprise you. Some will outgrow you. That is not a threat to your leadership; it is proof that you did it right.

You can never predict who your best leader will be five years from now. But you can absolutely control whether the environment you create suffocates potential or sets it free.

The Army's Paradox of Potential

The Army is built on an interesting contradiction: we openly acknowledge that war is uncertain, environments are complex, and people behave unpredictably under stress, yet we believe we can reliably predict human potential on an evaluation form.

Every evaluation in the Army includes a section where the senior rater assesses *potential*. This block carries enormous weight. It influences promotions, key assignments, schools, and ultimately careers. With a few checked boxes and carefully chosen words, we attempt to forecast who will succeed at higher levels of responsibility. The paradox is simple and prickly: **we know the future is unknowable, yet our systems are designed as if it is.**

Why do we think we can do this?

Part of the answer is institutional necessity. Large organizations require order. The Army must decide at scale who to promote, who to retain, and who to invest in, using limited time and information. Potential ratings give the system a way to sort people, manage risk, and maintain forward momentum. In that sense, predicting potential isn't about accuracy; it's about efficiency.

Another reason is that we confuse *current performance* with *future capability*. If a Soldier performs well today, speaks confidently, checks the right boxes, and fits the expected mold, we naturally assume they will continue to excel tomorrow. But leadership history, both military and civilian, is full of examples that prove otherwise. Some leaders peak early. Others struggle until the right mentor, environment, or moment unlocks their abilities. Potential does not reveal itself on a predictable timeline.

There is also comfort in certainty. Labeling someone as "high potential" or "limited potential" gives leaders a sense of control in an otherwise chaotic profession. It simplifies hard decisions and reduces ambiguity. But that comfort comes at a cost. When leaders believe their predictions are facts, they unconsciously narrow opportunities for those outside the favored group. Growth becomes gated, and the organization risks creating a self-fulfilling prophecy.

The real danger is not that we assess potential, it's that we **believe the assessment is final**. Potential is not a fixed trait; it is highly sensitive to culture, leadership, opportunity, and timing. When senior leaders treat potential as something to be identified rather than developed, they shift their energy from building systems that grow people to merely sorting winners from losers.

This is where the paradox becomes a leadership challenge. The evaluation system is not going away, and neither is the requirement to assess potential. But senior leaders must understand its limits. You're not expected to have a crystal ball and perfectly predict who's going to become exceptional. That's simply not possible. Your responsibility is to ensure that the environment you control does not prevent greatness from emerging.

If you accept that you cannot see the future, then the role of the senior leader changes. You stop trying to play fortune-teller and start acting as a cultivator. You design a culture where discipline is consistent, development is deliberate, mistakes are instructional, and opportunity is not reserved for a chosen few. In that kind of environment, potential has room to reveal itself—often in people you never expected.

The Army may require you to rate potential, but leadership demands that you **never let those ratings define the limits of someone's growth**.

If You Ain't Been Busted, You Can't Be Trusted

"If you ain't been busted, you can't be trusted" is one of those sayings you hear in the Army that sounds crude on the surface but carries a good amount of truth. It's not celebrating failure, incompetence, or misconduct, it's recognizing something deeper about human development. Leaders who have never stumbled, never been corrected, or never paid a price for a terrible decision often lack the perspective required to lead others through adversity.

Those who have been "busted" have felt the weight of consequences. They've experienced embarrassment, disappointment, and self-doubt. More importantly, they've had to decide who they were going to be *after* failure. Did they make excuses? Did they blame the system, the leader, or the timing? Or did they take ownership, adjust their behavior, and fight their way back? That choice is where character is forged.

People love redemption stories, and for good reason. Leaders who claw their way back from mistakes often develop humility, empathy, and resilience—traits you cannot teach in a classroom or capture in an evaluation block. They understand that discipline is not personal, standards are not negotiable, and failure is not fatal unless you quit. When they enforce standards later in their careers, it comes from experience, not theory. Soldiers can feel the difference.

There is a critical distinction here: being "busted" is not about misconduct that disqualifies someone from service or leadership. Some mistakes should end careers. This concept applies to *recoverable failures,* poor judgment, immaturity, overconfidence, or lack of experience. The mistakes that come from trying, stretching, and occasionally miscalculating. Senior leaders must be able to tell the difference. Development requires risk, and risk occasionally produces failure. Though I will always remain a huge fan of failure for its teaching potential.

Ironically, our systems sometimes punish the very people who take those risks. The Soldier who volunteers for the hard job, leads the complicated mission, or pushes outside their comfort zone is far more likely to make a visible mistake than the one who plays it safe. When leaders only reward flawlessness, they unintentionally select for risk-avoidance, not growth. Over time, this creates organizations full of leaders who look good on paper but struggle when conditions are no longer controlled.

Leaders who have been knocked down and chosen to get back up bring something invaluable to a formation: credibility and empathy. When they talk about accountability, they mean it. When they talk about recovery, they've lived it. When a Soldier fails under their watch, they don't immediately reach for the hammer; they assess, coach, and decide whether this is a moment to correct or a moment to cut ties. That judgment comes from experience, not doctrine.

This is where the concept ties directly back to potential. If you believe potential is fixed, then failure is disqualifying. But if you believe potential is cultivated, then failure becomes data. It tells you where friction exists, what systems are broken, and who has the grit to endure discomfort in pursuit of growth. Some of the best leaders in the Army were once the problem children—the ones who needed extra counseling, extra supervision, or a hard conversation in a cramped office. What set them apart was not perfection, but persistence.

As senior leaders, our job is not to shield people from failure, nor is it to crush them when they stumble. Our job is to build a culture where mistakes are acknowledged, lessons are extracted, and standards remain uncompromising. A culture that allows redemption without lowering the bar produces leaders who are both competent and human.

So when you hear, "If you ain't been busted, you can't be trusted," don't take it as an endorsement of failure. Take it as a reminder: **growth leaves scars**, and leaders without scars often haven't been tested enough to earn full trust. The goal is not to avoid failure at all costs—the goal is to survive it, learn from it, and come back better.

I can say this with complete honesty: young Private Massey was a snot-nosed, back-talking, arrogant punk. I cut more grass with scissors in full kit than I care to admit, almost entirely for behavior issues. My misconduct wasn't cruel or malicious; it lived in the "cheeky and fun" category, but it was still misconduct. I tested boundaries, ran my mouth, and assumed I was smarter than the system and the leaders around me.

What those moments gave me, though, was something far more valuable than a spotless record: perspective. I learned what it feels like to be on the receiving end of discipline. I learned how quickly credibility can evaporate and how long it takes to earn it back. Most importantly, I learned that accountability, when applied consistently and fairly, is not about humiliation; it's about azimuth correction.

Those extra-duty hours didn't break me. They slowed me down just enough to force reflection. They taught me that potential isn't about who you are at 18 or 19 years of age, it's about who you choose to become after someone tells you, clearly, that you're wrong. That lesson stayed with me far longer than any counseling statement ever did, and it shaped how I would later discipline, develop, and advocate for my own Soldiers.

Today, I'm grateful for those leaders who still, often unknowingly, saw potential in me. Not because they believed they could predict my future, but because they chose not to close the door on it. I don't think any of them looked at Private Massey and thought, *this kid is going to turn out great*. What they did instead was far more important: they enforced standards, held me accountable, and still left room for me to grow.

They didn't confuse discipline with dismissal. They corrected my behavior without writing me off as a lost cause. In doing so, they weren't betting on who I *would* become, they were investing in who I *might* become. That distinction matters. Potential isn't something leaders accurately forecast; it's something they protect long enough to develop.

Those leaders didn't need a crystal ball. They needed patience, consistency, and the discipline to apply standards evenly. In hindsight, that restraint, not prediction, is what made all the difference. Though I believe they really didn't know that is what they were doing.

Wrapping It Up

We are not fortune-tellers. No matter how experienced we become, we cannot accurately forecast who will rise to greatness and who will fall short. History, both personal and organizational, is littered with misjudgments: the "lost cause" who becomes an exceptional leader, the early star who fades, the arrogant private who learns humility the hard way.

The danger lies not in assessing performance today, but in treating those assessments as permanent verdicts on tomorrow. When we label too early and too finally, we limit opportunity, reinforce self-fulfilling prophecies, and risk suffocating the very potential we claim to seek.

Senior leadership, then, is not about identifying future greatness with perfect accuracy—an impossible task. It is about refusing to let our limited vision become a barrier to someone else's growth.

Hold the standard high and enforce it consistently. Correct behavior without closing the door on redemption. Create a culture rooted in discipline, trust, clear communication, and deliberate development, one that treats failure as data, not destiny.

In the end, your legacy will not be measured by how many future stars you correctly picked out on an evaluation form. It will be measured by how many Soldiers look back and say their potential was protected, not predicted, how many were given the space to surprise everyone, including themselves.

Because in a profession defined by uncertainty, the wisest leaders are the ones humble enough to admit: We don't know who will be great. But we can damn sure make sure no one is counted out too soon.

Chapter Nine

Invest in yourself

The Only Investment with Guaranteed Returns

> "If you join the military, you better walk out of your military career with at least a master's degree."

I've said that quote more times than I can count during my Army career, and I mean every word. There is absolutely no excuse for leaving the military without having invested heavily in your own education, especially when it's completely free. Good ol' Uncle Sugar will cover every penny if you're willing to do a little planning and a little work. If you play the game right, you can even walk away making money while earning your degree.

This chapter is about leveraging your time in the best way possible. Education is one of the few benefits the military offers that compounds over time, long after the uniform comes off. I'll walk you through my own educational journey, how I earned my Master of Business Administration, and the lessons I learned along the way.

And if you're willing to think bigger, I'll challenge you even further. A doctorate isn't some mythical achievement reserved for academics or ivory towers. It's attainable, even while serving, if you understand the system and commit to yourself the same way you commit to your unit. I'll show you how that's possible, too.

The truth here is simple: the Army will invest in you, but only if you're willing to invest in yourself first.

The Start of My Educational Journey as a Master Fitness Instructor

My educational journey truly began when I was assigned to a Regimental Training Institute as a U.S. Army **Master Fitness Instructor,** a title that sounds far more impressive (and dangerous) than it probably should. Some people spend their entire lives studying fitness, kinesiology, and human performance. Meanwhile, there I was, officially stamped by the U.S. Army as a *Master* of Fitness with exactly zero accredited academic credentials to support it.

That disconnect bothered me.

If I were going to walk around wearing that title, ridiculous or not, I felt an obligation to earn it in more than name alone. So I decided I would pursue a degree in exercise science to build accredited knowledge behind the label. Not because the Army required it, but because I did.

That decision marked the true beginning of my educational journey.

The first step was finding a college that actually fit my reality, not some brochure version of it. One requirement was non-negotiable: the program had to be **100% online**. The Army has a habit of sending me places with little notice, and I needed a school that could move when I did.

I also knew better than to pick the first school that popped up at the top of a search engine. I had a short list of deal-breakers. The school needed a physical campus, proper accreditation, acceptance of Federal Tuition Assistance, and a nonprofit university. After digging through options, I landed on a Minnesota-based university that checked every box and offered a fully online exercise science program, **Concordia University, St. Paul**. Not an Ivy League name, but it was exactly what I needed, and that mattered far more than prestige.

Next came navigating Federal Tuition Assistance. At the time, the system was called **GoArmyEd**, and "user-friendly" would have been a generous description. Like most things buried inside the Army's bureaucracy, the real secret ingredient wasn't brilliance; it was persistence. After plenty of research and guidance from others who had successfully navigated the process, I eventually figured it out and got enrolled.

To the Army's credit, the process has improved significantly since then. Today's **Army IgnitEd** system is far more streamlined and accessible. But the lesson remains the same: opportunities exist, but no one is going to walk you through them step by step. If you want to invest in yourself, you have to be willing to push through the paperwork, frustration, and learning curve to make it happen. I continued working on my education in **tandem** with my role as a Master Fitness Instructor, a pairing that fit together perfectly. But like most things in the Army, stability is temporary. Change was already forming on the horizon, new orders, a move, and a familiar shift in my career path.

Life as a Geographical Bachelor

The term *"geographical bachelor"* refers to a service member who executes a permanent change of station (PCS) while their family remains behind, often by choice, rather than committing to a full household move.

Around 2017, I was assigned to my new unit as a Readiness NCO, my first time in Bravo Company, 1-161 IN. The duty station was over 100 miles from our home. My wife and I decided not to move. We didn't want to rip the kids out of their school, routines, and friendships, and it felt like the responsible call. The plan, *and that word is doing a lot of work here,* was a short-term solution: I'd be a weekend dad, sleep in the office during the week, and we'd reassess later.

We were working a 4–10 schedule, so it didn't seem terrible on paper. The drive was about three hours, and I had zero interest in spending that time commuting daily. What started as a "temporary fix" quickly became the norm. Being an absent partner and parent is no way to treat your family. I knew we were resilient, after all, I had already put them through several deployments, and I justified this arrangement by convincing myself they could handle it.

I would never recommend this plan to any family. What we thought would be short-term turned into just over three years, and it was not sustainable. It put unnecessary strain on my marriage, my relationship with my kids, and my own mental health. Unfortunately, this way of life wasn't uncommon then. Moving is hard, especially when your kids are older or in high school, and many full-time Guard Soldiers were living some version of this same reality.

Instead of drinking my sorrows away during the weeknights I spent away, I made a different choice. I used that time to double down on school. What started as a coping mechanism quietly became one of the most important investments I ever made in myself.

I used every spare hour to get as far ahead as I could in my coursework. It wasn't easy. Much of the material was well outside my comfort zone, but as I said earlier, persistence can take you a long way if you have a clear goal. What began as a way to justify my "Master Fitness" title carried me well past a bachelor's degree and eventually into earning a Master of Business Administration through the same college.

Here's a practical lesson I learned about myself along the way: if I took a "year off" after finishing my bachelor's degree, I was never coming back. I already had momentum, I was used to the grind, and Concordia offered an additional $2,000 alumni grant, so after earning my bachelor's degree, I kept going. Sometimes the smartest move isn't taking a break; it's riding the discipline you've already built.

Another reason I stayed at the same school was that I already knew the educational structure inside and out. Sure, I could have transferred to a more prestigious institution, but that would have meant learning an entirely new university system, navigating different policies, registration processes, advising systems, and campus resources, on top of keeping up with my coursework. It just made more sense to stick with what I knew and focus my energy on my studies rather than starting over. As an added bonus, I never had to deal with resetting logins, passwords, or relearning how to use the online portal.

Getting Paid While You Attend School

It's no secret the Army supports higher education through programs like Army Tuition Assistance. If you're serving full-time, you're already earning a paycheck while working toward a degree. What I didn't fully understand early on, though, was how federal student aid could complement those benefits.

During my first year, I kept getting reminders to complete the FAFSA. I ignored them. My thinking was simple: if the Army was already covering tuition, why apply for additional aid? In hindsight, that was a mistake.

Submitting a FAFSA doesn't mean taking on debt. It simply determines your eligibility for programs like the Pell Grant and other forms of assistance. Grants are applied directly to your student account, and if your total aid exceeds your tuition and required fees, you may receive a refund. That refund is intended to help cover legitimate education-related expenses like books, housing, and transportation.

Tuition Assistance is typically paid directly to the school and helps cover tuition costs, while grants can offset additional expenses. When used together, these programs can significantly reduce—or even eliminate—out-of-pocket costs for your education.

In my case, the Pell Grant did most of the heavy lifting alongside Tuition Assistance. My tuition was covered, and any remaining funds helped offset the broader costs of being a student. Everything I received was processed through the school and fully within established guidelines.

That experience shifted my mindset. I stopped treating education as something I had to squeeze in around my career and started approaching it as a long-term investment—one supported by benefits I had earned through service. The key wasn't "working the system," but understanding it and using it the right way.

It's also worth noting that most need-based grants, like the Pell Grant, are primarily available at the undergraduate level. Graduate programs have fewer grant opportunities, though occasional scholarships or institutional aid may still be available.

Don't let excuses convince you that you can't do something. The most common excuse I hear when I tell Soldiers to use the free money available for education is, *"I don't have time."* That is a load of bull. You adapt, just like we all do.

If you have kids, you've already proven that point. You adapted your schedule, your priorities, and your energy without asking for permission. And in hindsight, it usually wasn't as bad as you might have thought it would be.

In my exercise science program, I learned about the SAID principle, Specific Adaptations to Imposed Demands. It's used by exercise science nerds to explain how the body adapts to stress to build strength or improve performance in a sport. That same principle applies to time management. When you impose a new demand—like school—you adapt, and it is not as hard as you make it out to be.

And let's be honest, there's usually one thing that gets sacrificed in the process: a small amount of sleep.

Now, that doesn't mean you run yourself into the ground or treat exhaustion like a badge of honor. Sleep still matters; it affects decision-making, emotional control, physical health, and long-term performance. The goal isn't to eliminate sleep; it's to manage your time with intent. That means cutting wasted hours scrolling reels on your phone, being honest about distractions, and setting non-negotiable blocks for both work and recovery.

Some seasons require tighter margins than others, but effective leaders learn how to balance effort and endurance. You don't win by burning out, you win by managing your energy as deliberately as you manage your time.

So, if you want to know when the best time is, **it is now!** If you haven't already done so, then get enrolled in school and earn all the degrees you can until your military career is done. Trust me, you will be glad you did.

Sobriety: The Absolute Best Self-Investment

I'm going to say something that won't make me popular at any unit happy hour: if you want to be the leader your Soldiers need, you cannot rely on alcohol as a crutch. Too often in the military, we treat alcohol like a reward, a social lubricant, or a stress reliever. I get it, it's been part of the culture for decades. But it also masks problems, slows recovery, clouds judgment, and erodes discipline faster than any bad leader ever could.

I'm not talking about avoiding a beer at a barbecue or a toast at a promotion. I'm talking about letting alcohol dictate your coping strategies, your leadership presence, or your decision-making. Leaders who lean on drinking to manage stress risk more than a hangover, they risk undermining the very culture they are trying to build.

During my years leading Soldiers, I learned that staying sharp, clear-headed, and fully present—not just for myself, but for everyone who depended on me—was non-negotiable. Sober leadership doesn't make you boring; it makes you reliable and deeply respected. It lets you spot minor issues before they snowball into major problems, and it ensures you're truly there in every formation, briefing, and conversation. Remember: you are not their friend who gets drunk with the boys to build rapport. That is the fastest way to erode your authority and lose your platform as a leader.

If you think about it, leadership is a high-stakes job where the margin for error is razor-thin. Every terrible choice, every missed detail, every lapse in judgment compounds, often with serious consequences for the mission and the people who depend on you. Alcohol reduces that margin even further by impairing judgment, slowing reactions, and clouding presence when it's needed most. Choosing sobriety, or at least disciplined moderation, isn't about being perfect or boring; it's about giving yourself the best possible chance to lead effectively and protect those who rely on you. It serves as another layer of professional body armor.

Now, I'm no stranger to making poor decisions under the influence of alcohol. Anyone who knows me, knows I have a drunken alter ego whose exploits could fill the pages of a novel. But as of this writing, I'm approaching three years of complete sobriety. That's right, I'm a total square. And I wouldn't trade it for anything. This is where I will say if you need help, please have the self-awareness, humility, and professionalism to seek it out.

I still attend formal military functions where alcohol is often the main attraction, but I quietly bring my secret stash of near beer, and no one is the wiser. It's my little harmless rebellion, and it keeps me fully present, fully in control, and still part of the team. Despite what most people who drink might think, you *can* have fun without alcohol, and, absolutely, you can enjoy life more fully when you do.

As far as investing in yourself is concerned, if you can find your path to leave alcohol behind you, it will most likely be the most beneficial investment you will ever make.

Physical Fitness: The Gift That Will Carry Far Beyond Your Military Career.

Now, since I was an exercise science nerd. I studied the principles, debated the physiology, and yet... struggled to practice what I preached. But I managed to apply a few key lessons that helped me chase what my wife calls my "midlife crisis goal." When she firmly said *no* to my motorcycle dreams, I went with the next best thing: Ranger School... at 43 years young!

If Ranger School at 43 taught me anything, it's that physical fitness isn't just about looking good on a fitness test; it's the foundation that allows you to lead, endure, and keep going when everyone else is ready to quit. Fitness isn't a checkbox or a weekend hobby; it's a daily habit that builds resilience, confidence, and credibility with the people who follow you.

I won't sugarcoat it: getting fit, staying fit, and pushing past your limits hurts. It's uncomfortable. It demands consistency, discipline, and sometimes sacrifice. But the payoff isn't just in the accolades, the promotion, or the bragging rights; it's in knowing that you can handle what you ask others to do. If you can't meet your own standards, how can you expect others to meet them?

The lessons I learned in exercise science and through personal experience weren't just about lifting weights or running miles. They were about **understanding the body, respecting recovery, and applying smart strategies to reach goals safely and sustainably**. Sleep, nutrition, and recovery are as critical as the workouts themselves, skipping them doesn't make you tougher, it makes you more fragile.

Most importantly, fitness is a **leadership tool**. Your Soldiers, peers, and subordinates watch you. Your effort, your persistence, and your refusal to settle for mediocrity set the tone for the entire unit. If you prioritize your body, you're signaling that you take your responsibilities seriously, you respect your profession, and you value your team.

Let's drop the political correctness for a moment. Do you want fit, lean killers on your flank, or a rotund, wheezing formation fighting both the enemy and its own lifestyle choices?

Truth is this: lean, fit Soldiers often earn respect from the moment they walk into the room. That initial perception matters. While actions and character will ultimately sustain—or destroy—that respect, first impressions set the conditions. Think of physical fitness as your first layer of professional body armor.

Subordinates, peers, leaders, and even our enemies notice it immediately. It signals discipline, self-control, and readiness before you ever say a word. On the other hand, carrying excess weight sends a different message, one that's just as loud, but far less favorable. It's the most visible nonverbal communication you have, and it's one you can't hide from. Your daily choices are already speaking for you.

The good news is this: you are not stuck where you are. Your potential is not capped by your current condition. Fitness is a choice, and so is change. Start by establishing a goal, commit to it, and get after it, because no one else can do that work for you. Set that goal and take action!

Most people call it goal setting, I call it **establishing impending doom.** Ranger School was my target, and I told my Training NCO to enroll me but set the start date for about two years out. Why so far? Because at my "advanced age," recovery takes longer, after every exercise, every minor injury, I need extra time. Those two years gave me a realistic window to prepare. Once my spot was reserved, there was no turning back. My goal was set. My impending doom was officially counting down the days. It was time to take action to make this goal a reality.

I didn't waste money on some fancy training program. I kept it simple and progressive. A plan I could easily follow. My first gate? The Ranger Physical Assessment (RPA). That became the focus of every workout, every session, every sweat-soaked morning.

Consistency mattered, but what mattered most was recovery. It's tempting to push hard and try to progress too quickly, but that's a fast track to unnecessary injuries. Slow, methodical, minor progressions were the key. Each small step added up to massive gains over two years. I won't get into the weeds of every drill or lift, I just know it worked. The results speak clearly: I earned the Ranger Tab, though it took a few tries in Mountain Phase, which I like to call "the extended stay" version of Ranger School.

Staying fit is about setting yourself up for life after the uniform. The same discipline, grit, and consistency you build in the gym or on the trail carries far beyond your military career.

I've seen it over and over. Soldiers who ignore their fitness while in service often pay the price later: chronic injuries, heart issues, obesity, and the frustration of realizing that their body no longer responds the way it once did. On the flip side, those who commit to fitness, not for the test, but for themselves, carry a freedom with them that retirement can't take away. You move easier, recover faster, your mind stays sharper, and the confidence you earned through discipline doesn't fade when your uniform comes off.

Fitness becomes currency for a better life in your future. It's about being able to pick up your kids without fear of throwing your back out. It's about being able to chase your grandkids, run a marathon if you want, or hike a mountain just because you can. It's about living a life where your body doesn't hold you back from doing what you want.

The Army can teach you leadership, tactics, and strategy, but only you can ensure your body and health carry forward into the decades beyond service. Fitness isn't optional. It's a lifelong investment, and the return on investment (ROI) pays dividends every single day of your life.

Life-Long Learner

One of the single biggest advantages you can give yourself, inside the Army or out, is the mindset of a lifelong learner. The day you stop learning is the day you stagnate. And stagnation is the enemy of leadership, growth, and success.

Learning isn't just about formal degrees, though I can't stress enough the value of leveraging every educational opportunity the Army offers. It's about curiosity, humility, and a refusal to believe you are all-knowing. Leaders who stop learning quickly find themselves out of touch, irrelevant, and ineffective. Soldiers respect someone who keeps growing, someone who asks questions, experiments, and seeks knowledge, not someone who hides behind their rank or title.

Life-long learning is messy. It's uncomfortable. It challenges your assumptions, your habits, and sometimes even your ego. But that's the point. Growth doesn't happen in comfort zones, it happens when you push, fail, reflect, and push again.

Here's the kicker: the benefits don't stop when you hang up the uniform. A mind trained to absorb, adapt, and improve will thrive in civilian careers, in business, and in life. The skills you build by constantly learning, problem-solving, critical thinking, and resilience translate to every challenge you'll face. The more you learn, the sharper your edge, the wider your opportunities, and the more respect you earn from the people around you.

Don't wait for someone to tell you it's time to go back to school, take a course, or read a book. Take ownership. Set goals. And don't just check the box, learn to dominate your field of interest. If you are like me, you take advantage of every moment you can get to learn something new.

I'm in the car a ton, hours every week just going from point A to point B. Audiobooks have been a game-changer for keeping my learning going. Instead of zoning out or letting the time vanish, I treat it like classroom time: leadership books, history, strategy, business—all of it. That's what I love about lifelong learning—it doesn't demand a desk or a formal setup. It's about squeezing growth out of every spare minute.

I get audiobooks aren't for everybody, but they're perfect for me. I honestly retain information way better when it's read aloud. Listening while I drive or hit the gym turns what used to be dead time into actual, useful learning.

There are multiple sources to get audiobooks for your continuous learning journey, I'll let you do the research to find the best service. Books, podcasts, webinars, mentorship, even casual conversations with smart people, all add layers to your understanding of the world and your place in it.

There's no shortage of things to learn, and I'd encourage you to keep seeking new ways to develop your skills, always pushing yourself to grow, adapt, and stay ahead. I want to reiterate something mentioned in the first chapter, *knowing* is the perfect blockade to learning. The moment you believe you already know something, you close the door on new understanding. Take the time to challenge your own assumptions about knowledge. Humility in the face of what you think you know is the real path to growth.

Time is your most valuable asset. Find the time. Use it. Even a few focused minutes a day compound faster than most people realize. Just like fitness, consistency beats intensity. There is no finish line. No medal or certificate can replace the advantage of curiosity, persistence, and the relentless pursuit of understanding. Keep learning. Keep adapting. Keep growing. Because the person who stops learning is the person who stops leading. And you are built for more than just "good enough."

Wrapping It Up

No one will invest in you like you can invest in yourself. The Army will provide opportunities, Tuition Assistance, training, mentorship, but it won't do the work for you. That part is on you. Your body, your mind, your skills, your discipline are yours to build, protect, and improve.

Fitness isn't just for passing a test; it's a lifestyle that pays dividends decades into retirement. Education isn't just a checkbox; it's a foundation that compounds over your lifetime. Sobriety isn't about being boring; it's about showing up fully present, making the right decisions, and leading without compromise. Lifelong learning isn't a luxury; it's the edge that keeps you relevant, adaptable, and respected.

Every choice you make—or avoid—echoes long after the uniform comes off. So stop making excuses. Stop waiting for someone else to hand you an opportunity. Set goals, embrace the grind, push past the discomfort, and take ownership of your growth.

Invest in yourself relentlessly. Do it smart. Do it consistently. And when you finally look back, you'll see a career—and a life—built not on luck, rank, or convenience, but on relentless action, discipline, and the courage to demand more from yourself than anyone else could.

You've got one life in uniform—and one after it. Make both count.

Chapter Ten

The Future of Leadership in an Unknown Future

Adapt or Fall Behind

> "Abandon certainty! That's life's deepest command. That's what life's all about. We're a probe into the unknown, into the uncertain." — Frank Herbert, Children of Dune

Leadership has always been about preparing for the unknown. In the Army, that used to mean training for the battles we could predict, conventional wars, standard operations, and clearly defined missions. But the reality today is different: the future is messy, unpredictable, and full of variables that no one can fully control. Political shifts, technological advancements, cyber threats, and global instability are rewriting the rules faster than doctrine can keep up.

This means the leaders who succeed tomorrow won't be the ones who cling to yesterday's playbooks. They will be adaptable, curious, and resilient, qualities we've explored throughout this book. Just as self-awareness and humility (from Chapter 1) allow leaders to learn from past mistakes and grow, future leaders must challenge their assumptions and pivot when the battlefield demands it. They'll understand that rank and title are meaningless without the ability to anticipate, decide, and inspire under uncertainty. They'll be comfortable making decisions with incomplete information, taking calculated risks, and owning the outcomes, good or bad.

The future of leadership demands emotional intelligence alongside tactical expertise. It requires the courage to listen, the humility to learn, and the conviction to act decisively when everyone else hesitates. Leaders will be judged not by how well they follow orders, but by how well they anticipate challenges, protect their teams, and turn chaos into opportunity. This echoes the trust-building we covered in Chapter 2: formations, public presence, and controlling the narrative aren't just for today's drill weekends, they're foundational for inspiring teams in dispersed, high-tech conflicts where decisions happen remotely and instantaneously.

Training, education, and personal development aren't optional, they are survival tools. The leaders of tomorrow will be those who continuously sharpen their minds, build physical and mental resilience, and refuse to settle for mediocrity. They'll be lifelong learners, willing to challenge their assumptions and prepared to adapt when the situation inevitably changes. As we emphasized in Chapter 8, investing in yourself—through education, fitness, sobriety, and constant growth, isn't a luxury; it's a necessity for enduring the uncertainties of future warfare, where mental clarity and physical endurance could mean the difference between mission success and failure.

One truth remains constant: your people will follow your example, not your words. The leaders who thrive in an unknown future will be the ones who have cultivated credibility, integrity, and trust long before the crisis arrives. They will be the calm in the storm, the clear voice amid chaos, and the steady hand guiding others toward success, drawing directly from the "panic azimuth" mindset in the Prologue, where finding direction in doubt becomes the ultimate leadership skill.

Peacetime's Hidden Cost

The future is uncertain. The stakes are high. History warns us: after World War II, rapid demobilization, budget cuts, and a shift to peacetime routines left the U.S. military understrength, undertrained, and under-equipped. When North Korea invaded in 1950, units like Task Force Smith were rushed forward—poorly manned, short on modern weapons, and lacking realistic combat training. The result was early defeats and heavy losses. Peacetime is wonderful, but prolonged peace dulls the warfighting edge. Without the crucible of real conflict, readiness erodes, complacency sets in, and the first shots expose vulnerabilities we ignored.

We risk repeating that pattern today. Extended periods without large-scale war foster a false sense of security. The absence of unrelenting pressure means fewer leaders gain the tough, unforgiving experience that forges true resilience. This ties into the discipline we discussed in Chapter 6: without consistent standards and proactive structure, complacency creeps in like unchecked uniforms or skipped formations. It also connects to the unlimited potential in Chapter 7—peacetime often labels Soldiers too early, stifling growth instead of cultivating it through recoverable failures and "busted but trusted" redemptions. To counter this, leaders must enforce discipline as freedom, ensuring that even in peace, teams build the grit and adaptability needed for future shocks.

Drone Warfare: A New Reality

I'm no expert on drones or drone warfare, but I wanted to open this up for discussion because it's reshaping everything we thought we knew about combat. For centuries, infantry doctrine has centered on **proximity**—you had to see, hear, smell, and feel the enemy to close with, engage, and destroy them. That principle of direct, physical confrontation through fire and maneuver remains at the heart of the infantry mission.

Yet drones fundamentally disrupt this equation. Lethal force can now be delivered from miles away by an operator at a screen, joystick in hand, eliminating the need for physical proximity that once defined close combat. A junior operator, or even a small drone team, can influence outcomes at ranges that used to require entire platoons maneuvering under fire. A single low-cost First Person-View (FPV) drone can strike with precision that turns tactical actions into strategic consequences, creating persistent "kill zones" where troops can't mass or move openly without detection. In Ukraine, drones now account for 70–80% of casualties on both sides, forcing extreme dispersion, saturating battlefields with surveillance and strikes, and making traditional advances far riskier and more attritional.

This doesn't eliminate the need to close with and destroy the enemy. It changes how we do it. Drones extend the kill chain, but drones are complementary, not replacements. They can enhance lethality by providing immediate, maneuverable kinetic effects, suppressing, disrupting, or destroying targets to support the maneuver element as it closes. They will not replace the well-trained Infantryman.

The lesson is clear: drones are force multipliers, not substitutes. Leaders who integrate them to enable maneuver while preserving the fundamentals of close combat will dominate. Those who treat them as a replacement risk being out of position when the screens fail and the close fight decides the outcome.

This shift changes leadership fundamentally. Drones compress decision timelines, remove geography as a barrier, and blur tactical actions with strategic consequences. A junior operator can influence global events in seconds, power once reserved for generals and presidents now rests with young Soldiers. Nations, non-state actors, and even individuals can project force with cheap, accessible systems. Future conflicts may begin not with armored columns, but with a drone from a truck or garage.

Technology will accelerate, drones will be faster, cheaper, more autonomous, integrated with AI for swarming, targeting, and real-time decisions. Yet no algorithm bears moral weight, no sensor replaces judgment, and no machine carries responsibility. Leaders must master the human dimension in an era where technology amplifies every mistake. This demands the communication strategies from Chapter 5: clear intent, battle rhythms, and verification to ensure messages land amid compressed timelines. It also requires the trust from Chapter 2—trust in subordinates to act on implied tasks, as micromanagement fails in high-speed environments. Setting conditions for junior leaders to decide at their level becomes foundational, preventing the "no implied tasks" mindset that sets teams up for failure.

Drone warfare lowers the barrier to entry, meaning superiority is no longer guaranteed by size, budget, or tradition. It's earned through adaptability, learning, and culture—echoing the lifelong learning and self-investment in Chapter 8. Leaders who prioritize education and growth will prepare teams to think ethically and execute decisively, even when permissions lag behind the pace of battle.

Real Conflict as the Ultimate Forge: Operation Epic Fury and the Iran Campaign

While prolonged peace risks dulling our warfighting edge—as seen after World War II and in the early days of Korea—real conflict remains the most unforgiving teacher. It strips away illusions, exposes weaknesses in real time, and forces leaders and units to adapt under live fire, compressed decision cycles, and genuine consequences.

As this book goes to press in 2026, the U.S. military is undergoing exactly that crucible in Operation Epic Fury, the large-scale campaign against the Iranian regime launched on February 28, 2026. Directed by the President and executed by U.S. Central Command (CENTCOM) in coordination with Israel, this operation has involved overwhelming air and missile strikes, naval engagements, and sustained degradation of Iran's ballistic missile arsenal, production facilities, navy, air defenses, and proxy support networks. Objectives include preventing nuclear weapon acquisition, annihilating offensive capabilities, and ensuring Iran's terror-sponsoring regime can no longer threaten U.S. forces or regional stability.

Whether one supports the strategic rationale behind Operation Epic Fury or questions its necessity, the reality is that the conflict is sharpening U.S. military capabilities in real time. In its opening phase, the campaign has involved sustained, large-scale joint strikes against Iranian military infrastructure, committing significant air, naval, and cyber assets. Public reporting indicates that key elements of Iran's missile, air, and naval forces have been targeted, and the tempo of operations reflects the intensity of modern multi-domain warfare.

This real-world forge builds the resilient, lifelong-learning leaders tomorrow's battlefields require. Units gaining combat experience now, recovering from setbacks, adapting tactics mid-operation, and hardening trust under fire, emerge sharper and more credible. Whether the conflict's broader aims succeed or not, these hard-won lessons will permeate future training, doctrine, and self-investment, ensuring the edge endures.

Operation Epic Fury underscores a timeless truth: the military's warrior ethos is honed sharpest not in routine or simulation, but in the chaos of actual conflict. Leaders must seize these insights—integrating them into training, discipline, and team development—to prepare for whatever uncertain future follows.

The Best Way Forward

In a world fixated on drones, AI, and real-time live feeds, the most dangerous oversight is forgetting that technology fails. Batteries die. Signals get jammed. Networks crash. Electronic warfare (EW) saturates the spectrum, turning GPS unreliable, drone links intermittent, and comms spotty. We've seen this play out vividly in Ukraine.

Russian electronic warfare has significantly disrupted many of Ukraine's precision-guided weapons and drone systems, pushing operators to adapt with fiber-optic links, autonomous navigation, and other low-signature methods. The intensity of the electronic and reconnaissance fight has also driven both sides toward greater dispersion, since visible or concentrated movement is increasingly vulnerable to rapid detection and strikes. When the high-tech layer falters, the battlefield exposes any force that relies too heavily on systems that can be jammed, tracked, or blinded.

Analog readiness isn't nostalgia; it's survival. Map reading by terrain association, celestial or compass navigation under stress, disciplined observation without augmented reality overlays, verbal clarity in radio-denied environments, and precise fire-and-maneuver execution—these timeless fundamentals endure when screens go black.

Leaders who can "kill the power," strip away the tech crutches, and still maintain command, control, and momentum will thrive in the chaos. This is **brilliance in the basics**, a philosophy that echoes the core leader attributes and competencies from Chapter 1: character to stay steady, presence to inspire without digital props, intellect to read the ground unaided, leading through uncertainty, developing subordinates in low-tech scenarios, and achieving the mission when plans unravel.

It ties directly back to Chapter 6's truth: discipline equals freedom. Rigorous mastery of the analog basics prevents complacency, enforces standards that hold under degradation, and builds resilience against the inevitable tech denial. The battlefield will always test you, through saturation jamming, cyber intrusion, EMP effects, or simple mechanical failure. If you can't fight effectively without screens, AI assets, or drone overwatch, you're already behind. In those moments, fall back on the panic azimuth from the Prologue: reset, reassess, and move forward with what you truly control—your fundamentals, your people, and your will.

Analog readiness is the ultimate insurance policy. It doesn't replace technology; it ensures technology doesn't replace you.

Wrapping It Up

We know we can't predict the future, but we can still prepare for it. The battlefield will always test humans first. Machines are tools, not replacements for intuition, presence, integrity, judgment, courage, and adaptability. If we focus only on what technology can do, we're already behind.

Train your people. Trust your instincts. Prepare them, and yourself, for a world where signals go dark, and discipline, training, and character are the only guides. This integrates every lesson: self-awareness (Introduction), trust (Chapter 2), communication (Chapter 5), standards (Chapter 6), potential (Chapter 7), and self-investment (Chapter 8) all converge to build resilient teams for uncertain futures.

The best leaders of tomorrow will blend the wisdom of the past, the fundamentals of today, and the foresight to adapt when everything fails. You can't predict every battlefield, but you can prepare what always matters: the people you lead, the choices you make, and your ability to lead when the world goes analog.

The future is uncertain. The stakes are high. Start preparing every single day.

Chapter Eleven

Final Thoughts

A First Sergeant's Final Azimuth Check

"If you leave your outfit today, is it better than how you found it?"

The intent of this book is simple: to provide new senior leaders with a practical springboard, a reference for what to expect, and some tools to incorporate in their first months and years in a new senior leader role. I'm writing this to capture and preserve the lessons I've learned over decades of service while they're still fresh in my mind. I hope that this knowledge reaches the leaders who will take these lessons and forge a future to inspire the next generations, helping them carry forward the traditions, values, and high standards of leadership that strengthen our teams and sustain our Army, or whatever organization you may be leading.

I also hope that strategic-level leaders, or those holding positions well above company command, will read these pages and gain a clear, unfiltered boots-on-the-ground perspective. When you are at the top, it's easy to lose touch with the realities Soldiers face every day: the friction we may encounter, the weight of doubt, the quiet erosion of trust when standards slip, or the untapped potential hidden in the "problem child" who just needs room to grow.

These lessons are invitations to consider when developing strategic plans. I urge you to embrace clarity about what you may not fully see from higher headquarters. Tap into your self-awareness to recognize where assumptions might blind you and summon the fortitude to challenge what you think you already know. Open your mind to the ground truth: listen intently to the junior leaders and NCOs who live these realities, seek their unvarnished input, and let it reshape your decisions. True strategic leadership demands humility, not thinking less of yourself, but thinking of yourself less—so you can honor the people who execute your vision and ensure the organization's strength flows from the bottom up.

When senior leaders stay connected, humble, and willing to evolve, the entire force becomes more resilient, innovative, and ready for whatever uncertain future awaits. That's how we carry forward the high standards that sustain not just our Army, but any organization built on people.

I have served as an Infantryman my entire career and am well-versed in the realities of combat from my era. Those days may be behind us, but the lessons we learned on the battlefield remain critical. Remembering them and applying them is the only way to ensure we don't repeat the mistakes of the past.

If you've read this far, you're either already feeling the weight of the seat you're in or you're about to step into it. I wrote these pages because I wish someone had handed me something like this the first time I walked into Bravo Company as First Sergeant, when the playbook I thought I had didn't cover the loneliness, the doubt, or the quiet nights wondering if I was actually helping these Soldiers or just making things worse.

Everything here boils down to a few realities I wish I'd grasped sooner. They aren't flashy. They aren't classified. But they're the things that kept yanking me back on azimuth when the world felt like it was spinning out of control.

Leadership isn't measured by rank, awards, or how many deployments you survived. It's measured by how you treat people when no one's watching. Your legacy lives in the stories Soldiers tell about you years later, especially the ones they share when you're not around. That conversation with the young Staff Sergeant who told me I was the bad leader in his story still burns. But it also changed everything for me. Every interaction plants seeds. Make sure most of them are good ones. **Don't stress too much about making mistakes; that's all part of the natural evolution of leadership.**

Trust is everything, and it's ridiculously easy to lose. You build it in the unglamorous stuff: showing up sharp to first formation, calling out good work in front of the formation, keeping your word on evaluations even when the weekend is short, enforcing standards even when you're exhausted. Let "good enough" creep in once, and you'll spend months—if not years—trying to claw trust back. Guard it like it's your last magazine in combat.

Discipline isn't punishment; it's freedom. Clear, consistently held standards cut friction, kill uncertainty, and let everyone focus on the real fight instead of wondering where the line moved today. That goes for you too. The battle rhythm you protect, the uniform checks you refuse to skip, and the personal guardrails you keep aren't just for the formation. They keep you from drifting into the hypocrisy you swore you'd never touch.

I rank this above all else: Every team member you lead has unlimited potential. You must cultivate an environment and culture that gives them room to grow into it. Stop trying to predict who's going to be great—we're all terrible at it. Some of the finest leaders I know started as problem children who needed extra duty just to learn how to shut up and listen. Others who looked like perfect Soldiers quietly faded into oblivion. Your job isn't to sort winners from losers early. It's building an environment where discipline is non-negotiable, mistakes are recoverable, feedback is straight and timely, and opportunity isn't locked behind a favorites list. Let potential show up. Some will shock you—in the best possible way.

Invest in yourself as if your future depends on it—because it does. The Army will pay for your education if you chase it hard enough. Get the degrees, grab the grants, keep learning even when sleep is calling your name. Stay fit—not just to pass the test, but so your body doesn't quit on you twenty years from now. Consider sobriety (or at least iron discipline around it)—it keeps your judgment clear and your presence steady when your people need you most. The moment you stop growing is the moment you become irrelevant. Don't let that day come.

And finally, the one that keeps me awake some nights: the future doesn't give a damn about our comfort zone. Drones, AI, cyber, shifting geopolitics—maybe even large-scale combat again—the battlefield is changing faster than any field manual can keep pace. Peacetime dulls the edge; we forget how sharp it has to stay. When the screens go black, batteries die, and comms drop, the only things left are the fundamentals: map and compass, cold judgment, disciplined execution, and trust in the people next to you. Train the basics until they're muscle memory. Build teams that can think and move when there's no time to phone higher up. That's how you win when everything else fails.

So, here's the straight talk, from one First Sergeant—or senior leader—to the next:

You're not in that seat because you're flawless. You're there because someone saw enough in you to believe you could grow into the leader your Soldiers deserve. Don't waste their trust. Own the hard calls. Shield your people from the bureaucracy when it breaks. Stay humble enough to learn from your own screw-ups. Keep investing in yourself so you can keep showing up for them. And when the chaos rolls in—because it always does—be the steady voice that hands everyone a clear azimuth forward.

So, if you leave your outfit today, is it better than how you found it? This is a simple "improve your foxhole" concept. Never stop improving yourself, others and the organizations you operate in. Use this to drive your initial approach to a new outfit along with all the other lessons we learned during our journey together.

Be the leader who can give your team a panic azimuth.

You've got this. Not because it's easy, but because you care enough to choose the hard right over the easy wrong.

Keep the standards high. Keep the faith. And when you finally hand off the Company Guidon (or Bastard Sword in my case), make damn sure the people you led are stronger, tougher, and prepared for whatever comes next, because you led them and gave them the panic azimuth they needed!

About the author

D aniel S. Massey is a retired Infantry First Sergeant of the United States Army, concluding a remarkable 26-year career defined by exceptional leadership, resilience, and an unwavering commitment to his soldiers and country.

Daniel enlisted in 2000 and served on active duty with the 5th Battalion, 20th Infantry (Stryker Brigade Combat Team) until 2003. Following a brief period in civilian life, he was recalled from the Inactive Ready Reserve in 2005 and mobilized with the Wisconsin Army National Guard for a 22-month deployment in support of Operation Iraqi Freedom, serving as an Infantry Squad Leader. He continued his service with the Washington Army National Guard, deploying to Iraq (2008–2009) as a high-threat military movement squad leader, Afghanistan as a combat adviser to the Afghan Security Forces (2012–2013), and Ukraine as a combat advisor to the Ukrainian Armed Forces (2020–2021).

Advancing through every enlisted infantry role—from Rifleman and Fire Team Leader to Platoon Sergeant—Daniel distinguished himself as a First Sergeant in the 1st Battalion, 161st Infantry Regiment. His tenure included leadership of B Company, HHC, and C Company, before returning to command B Company once more. It is incredibly rare for a First Sergeant to have led the same Infantry Company twice in this role. Under his command, B Company achieved unparalleled growth and exceptional retention rates, reflecting his deep investment in the welfare, morale, and professional growth of his Soldiers. His presence and legacy remain indelibly marked throughout the unit.

A lifelong learner, Daniel completed advanced military education, including the Sergeant Major Academy Master Leaders Course, Master Resilience Course, and Master Fitness Instructor Course. At age 43, he earned his Ranger Tab—a testament to his enduring determination and ability to overcome challenges later in life.

Daniel holds a bachelor's degree in Exercise Science and an MBA, blending his expertise in physical fitness and leadership with business acumen. He serves as an executive board member of the Highlander Association, a nonprofit dedicated to preserving the heritage and supporting the members of the 1st Battalion, 161st Infantry Regiment.

His service has been honored with numerous awards, including four Meritorious Service Medals, six Army Commendation Medals, three Army Achievement Medals, four Army Good Conduct Medals, the Master Combat Infantryman Badge, Combat Infantryman Badge, Expert Infantryman Badge, Ranger Tab, and campaign medals from Iraq, Afghanistan, and the Global War on Terrorism among others.

He was also awarded the Order of Saint Maurice (Centurion Level) by the National Infantry Association.

Now embracing civilian life in the Pacific Northwest with his wife and family, Daniel leaves behind a legacy of mentorship, operational excellence, and profound care for those he led. His story is one of steadfast service, continuous self-improvement, and the enduring bonds forged in combat, military service, and brotherhood that outlasts any war.

Endnotes

1. ADP 6-22, (2019). *Army Leadership and the Profession.* Headquarters, Department of the Army.

2. Heath, C., & Heath, D. (2008). *Made to Stick.* Arrow Books.

3. AR 623-3, (2025). *Evaluation Reporting System.* Headquarters, Department of the Army.

4. Willink, J., & Babin, L. (2015). *Extreme Ownership.* St Martin's Press.

5. ADP 6-0, (2019). *Mission Command: Command and Control of Army Forces.* Headquarters, Department of the Army.

6. ADP 6-0, (2019). *Mission Command: Command and Control of Army Forces.* Headquarters, Department of the Army.

7. ADP 6-22, (2019). *Army Leadership and the Profession.* Headquarters, Department of the Army.